The Silence of the Mind

Ilie Cioara

The Silence of the Mind

BOOKS

Winchester, UK
Washington, USA

First published by O-Books, 2011
O-Books is an imprint of John Hunt Publishing Ltd., Laurel House, Station Approach,
Alresford, Hants, SO24 9JH, UK
office1@o-books.net
www.o-books.com

For distributor details and how to order please visit the 'Ordering' section on our website.

thesilencebook.blogspot.com

ISBN: 978 1 84694 829 9

A CIP catalogue record for this book is available from the British Library.

Translation by Petrica Verdes

Design: Lee Nash

Printed in the UK by CPI Antony Rowe
Printed in the USA by Offset Paperback Mfrs, Inc

We operate a distinctive and ethical publishing philosophy in all
areas of our business, from our global network of authors to
production and worldwide distribution.

CONTENTS

I would like to introduce you to Ilie Cioara, a rare flower of humanity, a hidden treasure, a realized enlightened being, translated for the first time into English. His writings are a mirror of the beyond, of something that cannot be expressed into words: it can only be experienced.

This book is not meant to be read from beginning to end. Open it randomly, choose a poem and absorb it, meditate on it, let it become part of your being.

The words are just a finger pointing to the moon – not a distant moon, to be reached sometime in the future, but the miracle of here and now, unfolding before our very eyes.

Carry the book in your pocket throughout the day – when you feel overwhelmed and stressed – open it and read a few lines – it will bring you back to the reality of who you truly are.

As translator, I must have read parts of this book hundreds of times. With each reading I discover something new.

The original poems were written in almost perfect rhythm and rhyme. I tried to stay true to its content and message, rather than the form.

It gives me great pleasure to share this wisdom with you, the reader. May you discover within yourself the reality that this book is only pointing to.

The Translator

Introduction

This book is addressed particularly to all individuals interested in discovering the Sacred by practicing "Self-knowing".

Through these mirror-poems, written in simple words, easy to understand by everyone, we intend to expose the thinking activity of the ordinary human being, functioning as "ego" or surface consciousness. This exposure is realized with the help of lucid, all-encompassing Attention – an attribute of the Sacred.

As the ego is encountered with the flame of Attention, it suddenly ceases its activity – it becomes completely silent. In the peace of the soul or psychological emptiness, a new consciousness appears – as pure Energy – in which Beauty, Truth, Love are reflected as in a mirror.

All of these are revealed spontaneously, by themselves and through themselves, without any contribution from the knowing mind.

Such poems – read in a certain way – help us transcend the finite world, integrating us into Infinity. They are unlike any other genre of poetry. Ordinary poems have their inspiration in the limited dimension, where the poet lives. All these poetical creations, through their content, are addressed to fellow human beings living in the same limited dimension and influence them accordingly.

The countless stylistic metaphors frequently used in overrated poems can only confirm this statement. They have an intellectual, imaginary and sentimental effect, sometimes moving us to tears. But their beauty is only relative, just as all is relative as long as we function from the level of human conditioning.

Intellectual understanding is and will always remain limited! As such, a literary critic will never understand someone who only expresses into words what he experienced in another dimension.

All the poems in this volume tackle the same subject: the meeting with oneself, viewed from different angles. In this context, the repetition of certain words is unavoidable.

But, in "Self-knowing" words are unimportant. What is important is what we discover behind them, that is, an integration into the reality of the moment. Each such encounter with reality is and will remain unique.

Whenever one of the poems is being read, the repetition is only of the words. Each time, the experience of transcending from the finite into the Infinite will be newness, absolute freshness.

Each encounter, performed through simplicity, weakens the egocentric structure that we have built and whose prisoners we are, causing our unhappiness and the unhappiness of the entire world.

The frequency of the moments lived in this manner will finally demolish the walls of the ego. After this happy event, our being will be led by the Divine Spark within us, directing us through Love, Beauty and creative Intelligence.

The poems are followed by a prose version, in order to bring more light into the subject and into each life problem it deals with.

The manner in which the book is written expresses the reality of this experience. Each encounter with ourselves as "egos" represents a true window towards Infinity, melting us into the Whole, as complete beings.

Ilie Cioara

Listening and Watching

Be still, stop, be attentive – a total attention!
Neither past nor future, be with the present moment;
Between you and what you listen to, let thoughts, images
                                              disappear,
Be just pure listening, a whole being, boundless.

The divine instrument – observation – alive and
                                        crystal clear,
You listen and watch, outside and inside yourself;
The whole thinking is mute – a tomb-like silence,
There are no expectations, no ideal projections.

All these will create in you a perfect order,
Body and mind, the whole being, in a direct relationship,
Able to understand any life phenomenon
In a certain, real and profound way, as ephemeral as it
                                              may be.

Such a simple meeting is pure meditation,
Practice this all the time, in every circumstance;
Start and end with a total silence,
The whole being in harmony – in a timeless state.

This peace gives you an ever-renewing mind,
Completely detached from the old, integrating in the
present;
Psychologically, you are without center, boundless, you
are Immensity itself,
Able to embrace the Eternity of the moment.

Through these simple meetings, the old man starts to
crumble,
A crack appears in the egoic structure,
Through it, the accumulated energies start to leak and
disappear,
They were holding you prisoner from times immemorial.

The Liberation started thus is continued, in time, until in
the end,
When the "ego", the sad conditioning, perishes,
The Spark – the Sacred within us – returns to the Source,
Sooner or later this is everyone's fate: total Liberation.

Here lies the whole secret of knowing oneself,
Mystery intertwined with spontaneous action;
The only one which transforms, and finally liberates
The conditioned being from its degrading "ego".

Always remember that knowledge keeps you prisoner,
Be quick to understand its unintelligent nature;
Give all your respect to the moment – meet it with
humbleness,
Through it, wonders open into the Infinite world.

The clarity, accuracy and fluency of this subject, as expressed in verse, is so self-explanatory that writing its prose version seems more difficult and less dynamic.

"Self-knowing" is based on the simplicity of listening and watching, both the outside world as well as the inner world – as reactions of the knowing mind. Finally, outer-inner become one single movement.

The flame of Attention is the instrument which accompanies them, as a lucid flash of pure Consciousness, characteristic of the reality of our being.

Through this wonderful contact between us and the flow of life, made directly and spontaneously, the knowing mind – as past and future – is completely excluded. Thinking becomes completely mute. The whole mind is in a state of complete passiveness, where we don't expect anything, as a purpose or an ideal projection. The inner order, the psychological harmony from inside our being creates a natural wholeness – body and mind – an unchanging unity, able to have a direct relationship with any life phenomenon.

We can call such a meeting: the state of meditation. It can be realized in any life circumstances – when we are alone as well as, for instance, when we find ourselves among a noisy crowd.

The starting point for meditation is silence – it transcends the whole being into a timeless state.

The peace of the soul – without being desired or forced, as we have shown earlier – provides us with a new mind, integrating us into Eternity on present moments.

In this simple state of "being", there is no center from which we look outwards and no boundaries which set our limits. We are the Infinite in constant movement, unfolding moment to moment.

Through these meetings with ourselves, the egotistic

structure imprisoning us loses its resistance. Finally, a real crack appears in the shell of the "ego", marking the phenomenon of liberation. Simultaneously with this fortunate event – which comes as an unexpected surprise, uncaused by desire or imagination – the fragmented energies of the "ego" start to leak and fade away.

From now on the whole being is led by Intelligence, acting through intuitive impulses.

We must mention that the phenomenon of liberation or Awakening from the tyranny of the personal self is irreversible. It sets us apart from the rest of our fellow beings, by giving us a new outlook on life and a new mentality.

Sooner or later, each inhabitant of this planet Earth will have to experience this fortunate phenomenon. It represents a turning point in the spiral of moral evolution reached by that particular individual.

From that moment on, his personal evolution reaches a faster and faster pace, with massive eliminations of fragmented energies, accumulated since ancient times during our association with matter.

One day, in a moment that no one can foretell, the pure Spark, absolute perfection, will return to the Source of the Sacred, from where it descended millions of years before in order to experience the duality with physical matter.

Before ending, we need to remind that any advice on spiritual evolution demands that we put it into practice. By practicing it correctly, it will create beneficial effects, both on ourselves as well as on the world in general.

The whole process of knowing starts and ends with the flash of the passing moment. Let us therefore give the moment all our respect, by encountering it with a humble mind. Only in this way it will reveal the beauty of life to us, as well as the mysteries of the Infinite.

The Power of Emptiness

The "void" or "psychological emptiness" is a strange
phenomenon,
It appears spontaneously, in the pause between two
thoughts;
As the old thought ends its course and disappears,
Its end is the gate, natural silence ensues.

Insist in being with it, as much as you can,
The mind is completely silent, we are attentive – a clear
consciousness,
All meanings, boundaries disappear – us and the Infinite
are "One";
Practically, we have a new mind – always fresh.

Being in the pause – I become infinite!
It separates two worlds. I leave the limited world
And enter Boundlessness, through total melting;
The whole being is calm – a constant sparkle.

There is no time, no space – just everlasting Eternity;
I move in direct contact with life, in a permanent present.
I am Pure Energy, without motivations,
The simplicity of existence integrates us completely.

We really encounter Life only through this "now",
Free from the old, we are able to embrace the new.
All this beauty vanishes, when another thought appears,
It comes from the knowing mind – an old recording.

Let it play its game, do not oppose any resistance,
Encounter it as it is, without any purpose;
It will certainly disappear, and "emptiness" ensues again,
Another opportunity to encounter it practically.

We find the real meaning of Life through this "void",
It is a boundary line between the two worlds:
On the one side the limited, where the "ego" is the
master;
On the other, the Infinite, where Love is the master.

Emptiness also separates Light from the darkness,
The permanent chaos through struggle, contradictions
and conflicts,
From the harmonious being, equilibrium and joy;
The whole egocentrism perishes, by encountering the void.

Peace, divine order becomes our nature;
It changes our way of being, without effort or will,
Only through this psychological void, we become honest
and humane,
The Purity of the Energy – makes titans out of pygmies.

Let this "psychological emptiness" be your guide
In everything you encounter on your spiritual path.
If it is not the starting point, we easily get deceived,
Only through emptiness – we become Love!

The "void" or "psychological emptiness" is a strange phenomenon, which appears spontaneously in the pause between two thoughts. First, the old thought ends its course and disappears. At its end lies the gate, where natural silence ensues.

Persistently try to identify with this "emptiness" and dwell in it for as long as possible, by becoming one with it. In this circumstance, the mind is completely silent. In a state of Attention, we are pure Consciousness. When we have no motivations or meanings, there are no limits. The Infinite and us are melting into "One". In this state we have a new, fresh mind, which has no connection to the old mind.

In this state of "emptiness" or "psychological void" we notice that the whole being is perfectly calm and united with the Endless – manifesting itself as a spontaneous flash. Living in a real way outside time and space, we are constant Eternity, moving in direct contact with the movement of Life, in a perpetual present. By simply "being", we attain "wholeness"; we have a pure Energy, without motivations.

The real encounter with Life can only happen in this perpetual "now". When the old man disappears, we acquire the capacity to embrace the new, brought forth by the movement of Aliveness.

Life's beauty disappears instantaneously the moment another thought, as a reaction of the mind, invades this present and muddles its meaning. In this case, allow the intruder to follow its course. Do not oppose any resistance. We are just a luminous dot – a simple witness on the screen of consciousness – in stillness, we just watch what is happening, without any purpose, goal or ideal. When we encounter the intruder-thought in this manner, it disappears spontaneously, leaving the path open for the next moment.

The real meaning of Life is revealed to us only in the context of this "emptiness", as a boundary line between the two dimensions. On the one side lies the limited world, where the personal "ego" is the master, on the other lies the Infinite, where Love and Beauty create a climate of boundless Happiness.

Similarly, this "emptiness" separates Light from the darkness. The chaos we frequently encounter within the limited mind, caused by disputes, contradictions and conflicting states, is replaced by a perfectly harmonious being, manifesting itself as Joy and unlimited Happiness. Only in this circumstance, egocentrism disappears by simply becoming conscious of it.

This "psychological nothingness" makes us honest and humane. It radically changes our whole being, without efforts, desires or imaginary states. It represents the abyss, the tomb, where all the fragmented energies of the egoistic, obsessive and possessive structure disappear irreversibly.

Therefore, let us use it as starting point in each of our spiritual investigations. When "emptiness" is missing, any attempt of psychological progress can only result in deceitful imaginary states.

Let us remember that this attentive and lucid passiveness of the mind gives us the opportunity to encounter true Love and to identify with Divinity.

Each meeting with this "psychological Nothingness" is a true hammer blow to the structure of the "ego", whose author and prisoner we are. Depending on the frequency of these blows, we will, one day, experience the phenomenon of Liberation.

This fortunate event appears as a complete surprise. It cannot be desired, imagined, nor expected as a result or merit of a psychosomatic activity pursuing a goal or an ideal.

Calm and Relaxed

To everything that comes from inside, as well as outside,
As turbulent reactions, as imaginary forms,
Just be relaxed – watch, listen – in a perfect way;
Neither past, nor future. With a lucid Attention, you
                              encounter Truth.

There are no memory residues present in this meeting;
"Psychological emptiness" is the gate to infinite Love.
The Calm comes about indirectly, not by wanting nor
                              through imagination,
But by simply watching the turmoil of the limited "ego".

It was created throughout time, from ancestral residues,
Constantly traumatized through ideal impulses.
We watch it totally – without any goals,
This direct contact brings perfect quietude.

Physically and mentally, health is maintained through
calmness;
This necessity is constantly pursued.
Always attentive, without any purpose, we just watch
and listen,
Calm comes on its own accord – we are integrated into
Eternity.

Calm and relaxation cannot be something we order or impose through a pre-established method, pursuing a purpose or ideal to accomplish. Whenever such a method is present, calmness is relative, imposed by a well-trained will. In such circumstance, the effort takes place within the limited structure of the "ego", confined by its very nature.

In order to reach this calm, no previous preparation is needed. We can accomplish it in any life circumstances, wherever we are: in a quiet, secluded place or even in the midst of a noisy crowd.

Lucid and all-encompassing Attention is the only instrument needed, and this is attained spontaneously, by encountering the reactions of the mind appearing as effects to the challenges of Life in its perpetual movement. Therefore, in utter simplicity, we listen and watch, with our whole Attention, both our inner world and the reactions of the mind, as well as the impressions coming from the outside world.

In this direct meeting, everything that is encountered by the flame of awareness disappears in a flash; in the "psychological void" that ensues, a formidable energy is available, integrating us into infinite Love. Once this mystery is experienced, calm and relaxation follow naturally.

Let us add that this calm, relaxation, equilibrium or inner harmony comes naturally as a gift – when we correctly encounter the inner and outer noise and the imbalance with a spontaneous all-encompassing Attention.

As we watch the movements of the "ego" – the rays of Attention cause their disappearance, as well as the demise of their author. The state of perfect inner silence experienced in this manner creates and maintains both our physical, as well as our psychological health and well-being. Moral evolution is accomplished, as the mind melts into the climate of Love.

To conclude, let us always be aware of the movement of the mind, without pursuing any purpose, goal or ideal. We just listen and watch, with simplicity. This and nothing else! Calm and relaxation come on their own accord and, as it happens, we are integrated into Eternity on present moments of authentic experience and Happiness comes as a present from Divinity.

The Importance of the Moment

There is nothing static, nothing dead, nothing frozen
In the whole Universe. Everything is in constant
movement;
Even so-called still nature, in its profound essence,
Follows the same law of intrinsic movement.

Newness and movement go hand in hand,
They are inseparable, creating uniqueness.
The moment – the hand of the clock – is used into Infinity,
Caught in Eternity, through it, the whole is holy.

The moment is always new, and in fact always creative,
Constant newness through an evolutionary impulse,
Nowhere in the Universe is there repetition,
Or frozen, static, petrified phenomena.

If we want to encounter the new, we must be the same
                                                    way,
Without returning to the past, without following any
                                                patterns;
Therefore, the mind is empty of our whole past,
It neither runs towards the future, nor follows any
                                                methods.

It is simple! Just watch the moment – life as it unfolds
Nothing comes between us and its movement,
The narrow and limited ego doesn't intrude,
Creating analysis and imaginary falseness.

Such a meeting transcends us into Infinity,
In the newness of the moment, we become eternal.
Spontaneously, nevertheless, we detach, in order to meet
                                        the next moment,
Nothing is accumulated, nothing is anticipated.

The purity of innocence accompanies the present moment,
With each direct encounter, the being is creative,
A new world is born, where compassion and justice
Join hands with Love, kindness and goodness.

But this change of "being" is not performed through
desire,
Nor by thinking, operating through effort and will.
All of these are just the "ego", trapped in the dimension
of time,
Unable to create a real transformation within itself.

The instrument which never fails, unique in its efficiency,
Is an All-encompassing Attention, in close connection
With the movement of the aliveness; it has no center,
no purpose.
It does not pursue anything, nor is it concentration.

In order to understand the importance of the naked
moment,
You need to give it all your respect – forget the moments,
seconds,
Which happened in the past – they are mere ashes of living
experiences.
All that was – is always dead – an obstacle to this direct
encounter.

In the whole Universe, there is nothing static, dead or
frozen. Everything, but absolutely everything, is in eternal
movement. Even within the so-called still nature reigns the
same intrinsic law of movement.

Movement and newness, in perfect interconnectedness,
affirm themselves as uniqueness. In this context, the
moment represents the hand of the clock, used by Infinity
in order to record the movement of Eternity. It is always
new, as well as creative and transformative, in an

ascending manner, progressively.

After these overall considerations, let us see what is the real, practical and logical attitude towards the encounter with the moment, with life, the only approach able to perform a radical transformation in our psychological structure.

In order to be able to encounter the newness of the aliveness in its movement, we must come out and greet it the same way. Thus, we don't return to the past, to what happened, nor do we project ourselves into the future, in pursuit of an imaginary purpose or ideal to fulfill.

With a completely empty mind, we simply watch life as it unfolds. Nothing comes between us and the movement of life, in the form of images, opinions etc. Such a simple and direct meeting with the moment transcends us spontaneously from the finite world into Infinity.

And just as quickly, like lightning, we detach, in order to be free again, and therefore completely available to encountering the next moment. Nothing is anticipated and nothing is accumulated from the lived moment.

The purity, innocence of the mind is our constant companion, as each moment becomes an opportunity of creative "being". Through this way of "being" – as pure Consciousness – we ourselves create a new world in which Love, beauty, compassion and kindness become a reality positively influencing the whole of humankind.

We must underline that the different beliefs, ideals, desires and effort fueled by will do not operate real beneficial transformations. For, all these means are initiated and supported by the "ego" – a limited structure – unable to bring radical changes to itself. Please be aware and do not neglect this fact!

Practically, a mind conditioned in time-space cannot bring holy changes to itself, but mere changes on the surface. Or, all this superficial cosmetic surgery can only give an even greater importance to the "personal self" or "ego".

The merit for discovering this wrong path of straying from our real being is solely yours and it demands a lot of personal work, perseverance and a very high dose of honesty when encountering our own memory reactions. Do not accept anything that the author states, unless you have discovered the reality of these facts for yourself, which, through their own nature, cannot be contradicted or denied.

The infallible instrument we use, unique in its efficiency, is an all-encompassing Attention which, in its encounter with life, has no center and no bounds, it is neither purpose nor product of accumulation.

Each moment of life demands that we show it the whole respect deserved by the Sacred Reality, by completely eliminating the old past as well as the imaginary and uncertain future.

Joy

A feeling of contentment, enveloping our whole being,
Joy is a divine gift and fragrance of Love;
The whole being is overwhelmed by Its blessing,
Body and mind are one, in a state of integration.

Such a fulfillment doesn't have its source in the worldly,
Such as successes, desires, goals, which define the "ego";
In such circumstances, the result is satisfaction,
An ephemeral state, based on achievement.

The Great Joy has its source in the Infinite,
We encounter it in a real way, through "being",
Transcending, we unite with the Divine
As universal being, beyond the limited "self".

It is not attained through a search, a certain purpose or goal,
Nor related to a memory which once delighted us;
Joy appears spontaneously, when we are Oneness,
We are All and All is within Us – as One Reality.

Only such moments transform man and the whole
                                   humankind,
Only thus the whole world aspires to fulfillment.
It all depends on us – on each individual,
Inner peace separates us from the past.

The climate of harmony, achieved frequently,
Through a lucid Attention we become independent;
It is like a laser, dissipating any turmoil,
Its simple presence is, in fact, the realization.

Joy is a feeling of contentment of high intensity, completely
devoid of any conventional support or motivation. It
doesn't appear as duality, "me and joy", because this "me"
cannot exist anymore, for joy takes place in the dimension
of the Infinite. We can also call it divine grace, connected in
a direct, awe-inspiring way to the fragrance of Love.

Joy cannot be programmed or anticipated through a
certain formula. It appears spontaneously, when our being
is unconditionally integrated, when body, mind and spirit

are united forming a perfectly harmonious "Whole".

This simple union is, in fact, absorbed into the Great Whole, where us and Divinity are "One". The feeling of "me" or the personality is inexistent. Therefore, the complete absence of mental activity can also be called the state of transcendence or complete melting of the "ego" into the Immensity of the Absolute.

Frequently, we confuse Joy with the feeling of satisfaction. Satisfaction is always connected to a worldly support. An ideal, a goal or a purpose are its support and source. Associated with the world of the transient, satisfaction is similar to a bargain, operating according to the law of demand and offer.

In exchange for performing an effort for a certain period or distance, we hope that, at the end of the tunnel, we will find the success we have imagined, as well as the satisfaction of the accomplishment. This type of action strengthens and amplifies the domination of the "personal self", separating us even further from "our True nature" – divine in its essence and its manifestations.

Let us look at it from a different perspective. As we have shown earlier, Joy manifests itself spontaneously, when the intellect ceases all its activity. Let us extend our explanations in order to make it easier to understand the correct practice of "Self-knowing".

On a physical plane, we don't do anything accidentally. Each time we start from a well-defined center, we are aware of our goal or purpose, as well as the means we need to use and we direct our activity towards reaching the expected fulfillment. Our means are desire and effort, sustained by will, as a factor of accomplishment.

All these actions are, from start to finish, performed within the limited dimension of the human psyche. The accomplishment – as a result – brings us a momentary satisfaction, which is going to disappear and be dissipated in the next moment. Our day to day ephemeral existence unfolds in this manner. Its effects are very obvious.

The mirror of the world is in front of our eyes, inviting us to just look. That and nothing else! The simplicity of this encounter, without any doing, transforms us into pioneers, founders of a different world in which Love and understanding are transformative factors for the whole community.

Starting from the ordinary activity of the mind, operating within the limited realm of the physical world, we have reached the crucial point where we merely become aware of what happens on this plane of existence. That is all! In that moment of complete silence, using the attentive, lucid and all-encompassing observation, without any goals for the next moment – we have attained the state of Pure Consciousness.

Such moments transform the practitioner, providing spiritual fulfillment, and through him, also changing the whole of humanity. It all depends on us, on each individual. We are lacking nothing in order to accomplish this grand work of deifying the current human activity, which is in permanent conflict with the movement of the Aliveness as eternal freshness and newness from one moment to another.

No Possibility of Escape

When Love envelops you, there is no possibility of escape,
For you are limited, love is all-encompassing;
You – an "ego", in ashes, love is the burning flame,
You are a mere fiction, love is creative Essence.

Fleeting thinking is your sustaining source,
It stems from that which was, according to an old
                                        programming.
You, like your source, affirm yourself through
                                        fragmentation,
Whereas love appears moment by moment, integrating
                                        through being.

The first thought which created you – an egocentric
                                        impulse,
Everything revolves around you – a self-centered
                                        programming;
Love was, is and will always be Eternity,
It is part of the Sublime, one with Reality.

You are amplified through time, through any
                                        manifestation,
Always repetitive, you act according to your
                                        programming;
Love is beyond time – a timeless structure,
A different dimension, existential in itself.

You are always in conflict with yourself, with contradictory
                                        desires,
You have, in fact, many facets, each in itself ugly;
Love is harmony, beauty, kindness,
Through itself a master, always clarity.

Confusion and despair, hate and vanity,
Follow you like a shadow and create your identity;
Love is eternal light, a total attention,
Sparkling flashes of divine origin.

In all you think and do, you follow your own agenda,
This is characteristic of the myopic, small-minded "ego";
Love is unity, enough onto itself,
It completely fulfills us with its burning presence.

As you can see, there is no chance of being face to face
with Love,
Be honest with yourself, abandon all hope
Of meeting Sacred Love in its Reality.
Be humble, disappear completely – become a nothing!

You cannot speak about Love, for you cannot meet her
this way;
When you speak, it's just hollow words, you are merely
nourishing your "self".
If you see yourself as you really are, arrogant and proud,
Silence immediately envelops you – through it, you become
whole.

The whole Being – now Love – is one with Boundlessness,
Where everything is in harmony, through a different way
of living.
The Sacred, the Source of Existence, affirms that,
through purity,
We can destroy the "ego" and live in Unity.

From the state of Infinity – as absolute Love – we try to demonstrate to the "ego" – a finite structure – its whole meaninglessness and powerlessness when faced with the reality of aliveness. Therefore, when Love envelops the "ego", there is no chance for it to safeguard its existence. Here are the arguments proving the undeniable reality of this fact.

Love is creative essence, an all-encompassing flame, fueling itself.

The "ego" is a mere fiction – just ashes – always limited by time and space.

The source of Love lies in Eternity. Love is immortal and it exists moment to moment, always new, creating a wholeness of being.

Whereas the "ego" is fueled by fleeting thinking and both the ego, as well as its source, affirm themselves as fragment and division.

Love was, is and will always be Eternity, as an intrinsic part of the Sublime – one with reality.

The "self" came into being as a result of a selfish thought, which creates its continuity and, through repetition, it programmed its self-centered nature.

Love is outside time and space, it is also without cause. Therefore, love belongs to a different dimension and affirms its existence through itself.

Whereas the "ego" – created through time and space – enhanced its conditioning through endless repetitions and imaginary programming.

Love is perfect harmony, beauty and kindness; master of itself, it moves with light and clarity.

Living as "ego", you are always in conflict with yourself through contradictory desires; you have many facets, each expressing the same brutality characteristic of the "personal self". Confusion, despair, hate and vanity follow you like a shadow and define your identity.

Love manifests itself only as Light and, through flashes and sparks of divine purity, it sublimates the whole psychic climate and makes any form of shade and darkness disappear. Love manifests itself as unity and nourishes our whole being by its simple presence.

Whereas you, as "self" – in everything you think, feel or do – pursue a selfish purpose or agenda. Your whole nature, created through imagination, defines you as a small-minded, ugly, ambitious, greedy and arrogant entity.

From all these arguments, you can see for yourself that there is no chance for you to be face to face with Love. If you are even remotely honest with yourself, leave any hope of encountering Sacred Love. Be humble, become a nothing! You cannot meet Love nor even talk about Love, in any circumstance. And if you do nevertheless, it's just hollow words, without any practical reality.

But if you see your vanity and you encounter yourself in a true way, in that happy moment you disappear. In the silence that naturally ensues, the whole being becomes a fulfilled unity. In this state, Love manifests itself fully, united with Boundlessness.

The Sacredness – source of everything that exists – offers all of us the chance to dissolve the "ego" and, as completely free beings, to live in unity and complete happiness. In fact, this is our authentic nature.

The Listener

Each person carries within himself a cunning listener:
An arrogant intruder, annoying and nagging;
His presence obstructs listening, which is purity,
Complete understanding, clear serenity.

When real listening occurs, the whole being is passive,
Attentive, perfectly open, silent therefore inactive;
There are no expectations, nothing to be accomplished,
In its wholeness – alert listening.

Is it really possible to experience such a state?
You will find the answer within yourselves, after persistent
                                                    attempts;
Do not despair at any time, for in each of us are written
Endless possibilities – clear, certain and precise.

Entertain no doubts, put your whole energy
Into this crucial achievement. Do not reject
Anything you hear. Encounter everything
With an open being – be one with what you listen to!

If what you hear is false, the false does not affect you;
It passes you by, it does you no harm.
If what you hear is the Truth, in that Sublime moment,
The wall of the "self" is pierced – in you, there is a
                                            moment of light.

By persevering in listening, the old man starts to crumble
And one day – a surprise day – all mysteries are revealed;
When the individual is liberated, he attains Immensity,
The Supreme realization – being one with Totality.

A natural question appears: How does the listener come
                                                    to exist?
How does he create an erroneous way of listening?
He is, in fact, a fiction, which appears automatically
From the thought processes of the personal "self".

Notice how the listener becomes self-important
And regards the world with disdain and arrogance.
Behold, someone is speaking. He immediately barges in
Distorting every meaning. Listening stops.

When there is a listener who criticizes and accuses,
The individual listens to the self and acts through
                                                    the self.
The connection is broken, each encounter is empty,
Thus it is impossible to reach Truth or Love.

Knowing this, another question follows:
How can we escape from its influence?
Every time it appears – encounter it
With a total attention, without any imaginary purpose.

This silent meeting dissolves it, totally,
What is left is pure listening, integrated in the present;
Listening – watching are not different from one another,
They operate the same way – in every circumstance of life.

In order to explain more clearly what the "listener" is, we will first discuss listening, as it can be associated with watching and tackled in the same manner.

The right listening is performed through the unconditional passiveness of the mind, with our heart and being completely open. We don't anticipate any ideals and, therefore, there are no expectations to fulfill any result.

The lucid, all-encompassing and spontaneous Attention is the only instrument offering the possibility to correctly make this experience. Intellectually, it is easy both to explain and understand listening.

Yet, practicing this simple non-action can encounter several difficulties which, with a little persistence, can be easily overcome. Each individual has the capability to completely fulfill this psychological attitude, absolutely necessary in the adventure of knowing our own being.

Therefore, we listen and watch, with our full attention, both the movement of the external world as well as the world of thoughts, images, emotions etc. The simplicity of the contact with everything we hear or see creates the passiveness of the mind.

In this state of stillness, the whole being, in perfect oneness, in a timeless state, watches, listens and understands perfectly, by living experience, without creating any memory baggage. Through understanding, transforming action stems spontaneously and undermines the authority of the personal ego.

Let us mention an example of listening which is deeply

significant. Here we are, for instance, listening to someone who talks and talks – mentioning all kinds of miscellaneous facts: good or bad, real or imaginary facts, truth and lies, according to the programming of the person's mind. All of these flow through us, like the water of a river, without any obstacles. It is a simple way of listening: the mind, attentive and lucid, is in a state of passiveness. The real, true things determine us to live them and feel their reality. The untrue, false things pass through us without affecting us in any way.

Let us come back to the subject of this poem: the listener.

In the moment, as the challenge of life demands a state of attention from us, an intruder appears! This intruder analyzes, judges, interprets according to his own knowledge, accumulated through culture, experiences, past events etc. Therefore this apparition – the listener – in a ceaseless activity, makes listening impossible. Fueled by old experiences and knowledge, through interpretation it distorts the newness and freshness of life in constant change from one moment to another.

Because of this undesirable intrusion, we are unable to encounter the beauty of the aliveness in its eternal movement, nor creative Love with its priceless riches.

Also because of this unwanted fiction, we are not able to encounter happiness without any cause, to which, consciously or unconsciously, each inhabitant of planet Earth aspires.

A natural question follows: What do we need to do in order to get out of this dead-end situation? Nothing or almost nothing! Completely identified with the flame of attention, we just listen to and watch the movement of this fiction, without pursuing any goal or any purpose.

This simple meeting with the annoying intruder spontaneously disintegrates it, without leaving any traces. In the psychological void that presently ensues, we are attracted into the Sphere of the Absolute, we become one and melt with it, thus discovering the divine reality of our being.

But let us explain this subject from a different angle.

"Self-knowing" is set into motion by the reactions of the conditioned mind, under the name of listener or knower. When faced with the flame of attention, this intruder dissolves instantly. In the void thus created, all that remains is all-encompassing pure listening or pure watching. In this circumstance, we manifest ourselves as a state of pure Consciousness, without cause and timeless.

Knowing is Boundless

If life is movement, newness each moment,
Knowing, too, has the same quality;
Boundlessness envelops both,
They are closely connected, expanding the being into
Infinity.

Through every contact with the existence in movement,
We encounter Eternity, in the dying moment;
Leaving the path open for the next moment,
We are always in a state of Timelessness.

If the Eternal wasn't already within us, we would not
                                        know Eternity,
It is always present, when we are in harmony;
Attention is the instrument, the divine tool,
With its ray of light, it dissipates all the chaos.

Each such encounter with the limited "ego"
Transcends us, without effort, into the great Infinity;
Therefore, knowing takes us eternally into Boundlessness,
This is its purpose, as a natural fulfillment.

Finally, the "ego" perishes – the Sacred becomes free,
It returns to the Source, where it becomes integrated;
Thus, "self-knowing" loses its purpose,
Without "self", what is there to know? All that was has
                                        disappeared.

Watching thus, it all comes to an end by itself, effortlessly,
The road is long, the path is narrow.
Our duty is to meet the boundless in the moment,
To disintegrate the "ego", with its deceitful fantasies.

This is our fate, as long as we live on this Earth,
To destroy, ceaselessly, our ties to the "ego",
Which holds us prisoners from times immemorial
And to embrace the rhythm of life, integrated in the
                                        moment.

"Self-knowing" is based only on certain and real facts, accessible to any human being in his natural capacity of understanding.

Here is a first fact related to this subject: Life manifests itself as reality in perpetual movement and, as such, newness from one moment to another. Therefore, the aliveness, through its very existence, is, in its nature, movement and freshness which never repeats itself.

Knowing this aliveness can only have the same characteristics; both melting together within the essence of the Infinite.

This way, if the meeting with life is real, in that moment, our being is integrated into Eternity. Immediately afterwards, it becomes detached, leaving consciousness free for a new contact with life, whose freshness and movement differs from the previous moment.

If Eternity weren't already within us, this meeting with the boundless and the everlasting would be impossible. This statement can be immediately proved by practice.

It is sufficient to face any of the reactions of the mind with our all-encompassing attention and we will see them disappear; in the psychological void thus created, harmony ensues. This state of "being" represents the communion between our whole being with the Absolute.

Therefore, knowing – if correctly applied – leads us each time into Boundlessness, in which we melt spontaneously. This is the purpose of our existence on Earth.

Depending on our passion for the truth, after a long period of living in both dimensions, the physical as well as the astral world, after a succession of lives, the energies of the "ego" are eliminated. In this fortunate event, the Sacred within us returns to the Source of Light, from where, millions of years ago, it started its difficult journey in order to experience the world of matter.

From this moment on, "Self-knowing" has no purpose anymore, because the "personal self", the generator of all the causes which brought us again and again in the form of this world, no longer exists.

The road is nevertheless very long and the path very narrow in the beginning. But the thirst, diligence and passion of the person who stumbles across this truth widens it, practicing day and night, without a moment's rest.

As long as we live tied to this earth through the body, there is nothing more valuable or useful to accomplish than the detachment from the slavery of the "ego". The simplicity of this knowing is within our grasp and it invites us to use it in confidence. The time of deceit has already taken too long; its results are too obvious to keep hiding and ignoring them.

In the beginning of this third millennium, reality requires a strict revision of all the practices which brought humanity into its present state of chaos.

Our times demand that we use a different approach to life, in which Love and Intelligence – as a result of personal discovery – can manifest its beneficial influence, so that human beings find the divine within themselves.

The Struggle of the "Ego"

It is not easy to demolish, to dissolve it structure,
It was formed many centuries ago and it has a tough shell;
Violence, cunning, hatred are its main characteristics,
A ferocious egocentrism is its permanent companion.

You cannot fight it through will or force,
For will is the "ego" itself, a form of nourishment;
Any effort makes it stronger and gives it more energy,
Man becomes even more possessed, the degradation is
                                              even greater.

Neither hopes, nor ideals, nor deceitful beliefs
Contain within themselves the seeds of change and
                                              renewal;
All of these are affirmations of the "ego",
Able to give it life, an even greater distortion of reality.

Only a simple encounter makes the "ego" grow weaker,
There is no purpose to pursue and no expectations;
It is a direct meeting – in the moment,
Just listen and watch all its activity!

When the "ego" starts to crumble, its security is
                                              shattered,
Angry, it laments its own fate;
Through cunning, it permanently tries to prove
How unnatural it is for man to be integrated.

Do not listen to it at all, do not believe it,
The simplicity of the encounter dissipates its power;
By persistently watching and listening ceaselessly,
Day by day its inner force becomes weaker.

Encountering it moment by moment are true blows to
the "ego",
Which will once pierce its wall and its stronghold;
It becomes simpler, when its fragmenting energies
Start to fade and disappear...

Day and night, ceaselessly, conscience becomes empty
And finally, the pure Spark ends its journey;
Completely free from its difficult prison,
Triumphantly it returns to the Sacred Immensity.

It is not easy to fight and dissolve the "ego", which
terrorizes our whole life. It was formed thousands and
thousands of years ago and it excels through its toughness
and cruel savagery. Ambition, greed, pride, hate and
violence are its main features, and its persistent goal is to
satisfy its ruthless egocentrism.

Any direct confrontation with the "ego" is destined to
fail, for desire, will and effort, or any kind of struggle are
its characteristics; they nourish its activity. Hope and faith
are also manifestations of the "ego", as well as everything
it imagines as a purpose or ideal to fulfill.

In order to avoid any ambiguity or shadow of doubt, let
us explain in more detail. A well trained will or a strong
faith, for instance, can create some changes in the mental
structure, which is in fact the "ego", but these are mere
cosmetic, superficial changes. Its core remains the same,
with a further degradation – the deceitful mask of the
hypocrite, who tries to camouflage his inner ugliness.

After the individual mind – dissatisfied with itself – has
tried all sorts of methods, analyses, faiths, in order to create
behavioral changes in itself, eventually it sees its own

powerlessness and refuses to move any further. Thus, in this state of passiveness, the key to overcoming itself is suddenly revealed.

In silence, a new mind, immense, boundless, accompanied by pure energy and light, envelops our whole being. From then on, every movement of the "ego" is automatically dissipated, without any intervention from the experiencer.

The inactivity of the mind, the lucid attention and the simplicity of the encounter with the movement of life represent, in fact, the death of the ego.

As the ego sees its authority being endangered, it becomes even more active. Sometimes it becomes violent, sometimes it laments and then, through cunning, it tries to persuade us of the complete uselessness of this path. It doesn't cease telling us that being integrated into Infinity is unnatural and that pleasure and personal satisfaction are more suitable to human nature.

To all these attempts, we answer with a definite NO. Make no compromises with the ego, no matter how touching and convincing its attitude and interventions are.

The simplicity of the meeting with the chaotic movement of the ego represents a true blow to the stronghold preserving its content and fragmented energies.

One day, which no one can foretell, its protective wall will crack. This is the beginning of liberation or Awakening. Through this opening, the content of the vessel preserving its false values and its long imaginary existence starts to leak and dissolve.

Finally, the pure Spark – the human being's true nature – freed from all the layers of matter, triumphantly returns to the Divine Source, to its home.

Be Still for a Moment and Ask Yourself

Be still for a moment and ask yourself: why do you run
                                    towards the past?
What is the point of reliving the moments which are
                                    already gone?
All that is old has no value in the present,
It is but a fantasy, empty and deceitful.

Why do you run towards the future? Do you believe
                                    it is new?
It is but another deceit – its source, the same "ego".
The projection into the future is old as well,
It comes from the same source: the memory baggage.

Therefore, the past or the future are not to be sought,
Through them, the Sacredness of life will never reveal
                                    itself;
It is always newness in the incoming moment,
It demands of us that we encounter it with the same
                                    freshness.

Let us be aware of ourselves all the time, of our wandering
                                    thinking –
Absurd and selfish in its mechanicalness –
It always wants to relive the moments it enjoyed
And to banish the unpleasant moments far away in
                                    the past.

Life, in its flow, brings us joy and pain,
They come together and can be found everywhere;
If our understanding is distorted, according to our own
                                                    prison,
The same "self" and its deceitful values is to blame.

The newness of life can only be encompassed in one way,
When we are aware of ourselves, without any purpose
                                                    in mind;
We are pure energy, open to the present moment,
This is the only way to encounter Absolute Reality.

In such a state, we are open to everything,
Without any fears or excesses fueled by the ego.
Man is wise when, free from his "self",
He becomes one with the Infinite through non-action.

The secret meeting happens in simplicity,
By eliminating all that was, we live in the new,
With a clear-lucid mind, we watch everything that comes
In its natural movement – we are the eternal divine.

Our functioning as complete beings, present in the
incoming moment, is closely connected to the correct
understanding of life.

For our natural state is that of moving and acting as a
complete whole – body and mind in perfect union. For this
reason it is necessary to constantly ask the restless mind,
wandering pointlessly: Why do you run towards the past?
What is the point of reliving dead moments? These facts

and events were once real and alive experiences; when they are recalled again in the present, as mere images, they are empty and deceitful, therefore worthless.

Why do you run towards the future? Do you think the projection into tomorrow is newness? Not at all. It is just another form of deceit. Its source is the "ego" structure as well. Projecting into the future is just as old, for it originates from the memory baggage.

Therefore, both the past and the future are illusory states; in the present moment, they are mere anachronisms preventing us from understanding the reality of the aliveness, absolute freshness from one moment to another.

How can we free ourselves from the past and the future? It is all very simple! With a lucid, all-encompassing Attention, we will watch every reaction of the mind, without pursuing any purpose or goal. Everything we encounter in such a manner disappears; in the void which appears spontaneously, an unlimited energy is available at our fingertips and we are able to understand the absolute Reality through a direct experience.

In this state, we acquire a great sensitivity and everything that life brings forth in its natural flow is being regarded and appreciated with love and kindness.

Man is truly wise only when, detached from his selfish "self", united with Infinity through non-action and an aware passiveness of the mind.

This mysterious encounter is accompanied by simplicity. Once the past has disappeared, we are integrated in the now and, with a clear and lucid mind, we watch everything that comes as constant freshness from one moment to another.

To conclude, let us remember the necessity of asking ourselves continuously whether, in the present moment, we are or we are not a complete being.

The thought traveling to the past or to the future fragments our being. Simply exposing the intentions of this thought makes it disappear. Only thus we are a whole person and we function as an intelligent being; through our act of living we create another world, different from the one humanity lives in at the moment.

The Mystery of Silence

Life is like a running river, in a constant renewing flow, determined by the Universal Law of movement. Originating from eternity, it flows towards eternity in a perpetual change.

Nothing and no one can stop it and cannot change its natural flow, determined by its own reality.

If this statement is in accordance with the undeniable truth, we ask ourselves: What is our relationship with life? Do we regard it as something separate from us? Or are we just lying on its bank, watching the river as mere spectators? Or do we throw ourselves into it and flow with it?

When we are integrated into life, when we are one with life, we watch all the events as they come, without opposing any resistance. We want nothing else except what is, in fact, in that particular moment.

In the quietness that follows naturally through the silence of the mind, we receive intuitive impulses from life, as to what we need to do in order to encounter the incoming moment in a correct manner.

Therefore, our encounter with the alive and active present is a movement without cause, in which the "me" with its whole conditioning is absent.

This direct, simple and spontaneous meeting is the only modality of coming into contact with the Truth.

In this circumstance, life's mobility and freshness guides us with wisdom. The "ego" has completely disappeared;

there is no desire nor aspiration, nor ideal.

The wise man lives only in the present, content with everything that life brings forth, without aspiring to or wanting anything else than what he has in the moment.

The richness and charm of existence consist in that complete and utter happiness provided by the stillness of the mind, which overwhelms our whole being through impulses of transformative Love.

***

If man discovered the reality of his own being, any life problem would be solved in the happiest way possible. And the inter-human relations would create a real paradise on this planet.

Perfectly conscious, I see the emptiness of this world directly and my mind becomes silent. I have no choices, not even at the level of understanding of this limited mind. In the silence that ensues, the mystery reveals by itself its secrets to us.

The whole being expands to infinity. A light such as we have never experienced before envelops us and heals us. Out of time and space, we have a pure consciousness – in perfect union with the Supreme Being.

All of these demonstrate that the alive within us is, in its essence, immortal. It has no beginning, no end, it never sleeps, being therefore always awake.

This is the final result of the correct practice of "Self-knowing".

***

How could this small shell, which is the human mind, embrace and comprehend the immensity of the ocean of

Cosmic Energy?

Nevertheless, this audacious "ego" persistently affirms that he knows what God is, what is creative Love, immortality etc.

More so, it states and even offers solutions to tackling and solving the great problems that challenge humankind.

Yet this "ego" is not aware of one thing: that its own presence creates the whole tragedy and suffering on the entire surface of the Earth. It is the human being's main and only enemy. Its fictitious, chaotic and misleading movement generates and maintains the human misery and suffering.

But when a ray of light, emanated by Pure Consciousness, pierces the limited shell of the mind and exposes its whole fiction, this mind becomes humble and silent.

***

I have strayed and wandered for many years, through various searches, practices, gathering information etc. I have followed wrong paths as well – true stupidities.

To you, my friend and travel companion, this perspective is offered, that through a direct experience you discover from the start the direct way of encountering the Truth.

It depends solely on you to meet this Reality, which categorically excludes egoistic duality. The means used in this sense are: an all-encompassing attention, watching and listening.

Just watch everything that appears on the screen of surface consciousness, such as: thought, image, desire, fear etc. The simplicity of the encounter dissipates them spontaneously, together with the whole structure of the "ego".

We instantly forget the success of one moment and, just as fresh, we encounter the next moment. In this way we eliminate, one by one, all our psychological traumas caused by this existence.

Only thus you become, in a real way, the Master of your own life, simultaneously with the demise of the egoic fiction.

***

As I have been once dominated by different patterns of thinking as well, I completely understand my fellow beings, conditioned by the social consciousness of the environment where they were born and received their education. The fanaticism of the religious faithful, the arrogance of the philosopher and the ego of the methodist are only a few of the thought patterns which are difficult to abandon, but not impossible.

Let us not generalize these apparent difficulties! In my discussions with several people interested in "Self-knowing", I was often told that: "I cannot accomplish this simple meeting with myself!" This "I cannot" – a reaction of our own ego – must never be uttered or pronounced, because by simply accepting it, we become powerless.

***

Can thinking be silent, such as a flower, completely open, letting the beneficial rays of the Sun envelop her and still, when some form of communication is needed, to respond in a natural way with a wholeness of being?

In fact, this is what life asks of us ceaselessly – to respond only when such a response is needed. The rest of the time, the being should be silent and watch in all serenity.

***

Enlightenment is a surprise phenomenon, opening the way to divine greatness for the ordinary man. The phenomenon is accompanied by two profound changes, namely: the crumbling of the "ego" and the transcendence of being from the finite into the Infinite world.

This fortunate event is not a product of the knowing mind, nor of imagination, nor of effort or will used to fulfill a purpose or ideal.

No one can offer us enlightenment. No saint, master or teacher can give it to us in any shape, way or form.

Enlightenment is the price of your work on yourself, and the psychological void represents every time the starting point as well as the completion of each action.

Once you have discovered true life, it transforms you, and through it, it transforms the whole humanity, for in the Great Whole – real essence through itself and by itself – everything that exists forms a unique, compact, homogenous mass. The transformation of one part naturally influences the whole.

Pure Listening

It is not easy at all to listen with purity;
Such a feat demands a lot of simplicity.
No thoughts, desires, purpose, feelings or images,
Have any reason to exist within the flow of our life.

The mind is completely silent, detached from the past,
Knowledge loses its importance from the very start;
The whole being is a flame, spreading light
Into the Boundless – everything becomes integrated
                                            and whole.

There is no "me" and listening, any duality is excluded,
The death of the "ego" – is the secret of encountering reality;
In fact, we are pure listening, in its very essence,
Sounds go right through it, without any resistance.

A state of superconsciousness and absolute attention,
A sacred stillness, in a perfect order.
To put it in other words, it is the "psychological nothingness",
It is the ear that listens and understands directly.

In such a state, our life is fulfilled,
Everything that "is", as well as what comes, becomes
                                            perfect through us –
In total abandonment, the being is completely open,
Encompassing everything within itself – a Perfect
                                            Understanding.

Thus, encountering the Reality of the moment,
The individual finds true life, through a direct
                                    experience,
Where there are no contradictions, no complications;
Everything is welcomed as it comes, without traumas
                                    or reactions.

Without toil, simply attentive, we have discovered by
                                    ourselves,
That by eliminating the past – everything we have
                                    gathered throughout time –
With a completely new mind, we will encompass only
                                    what is new,
Which affirms itself through itself, in its essence.

Watching is approached in the same way, without any
                                    difference,
The same phenomenon occurs, integrated in our being.
Watching and listening – in this manner,
In one moment we transcend into a different reality.

Spontaneously, we become immense, part of Eternity,
A perfect union – there is no more personality.
Happiness comes as a gift from the Great Love,
Purity – a witness to this great Liberation.

It is not easy at all to listen with a purity of the mind, either
to the noises coming from the outside world, or to the
movements caused by our inner world.

In this passiveness of the mind, knowledge loses its

importance from the very start. Therefore, no thought, desire, purpose, emotion or image has any reason to be pursued. Attentive and lucid, the whole being is like a flame, spreading light, extended into Infinity.

In this direct experiment, there is no duality, such as "me", the listener and listening. We are just pure listening, in which the "me", as listener, is completely absent and the noises that pass through it encounter no resistance.

We can also name this state – the state of Pure Consciousness or "psychological Nothingness", or a simple ear which is content to just listen and nothing else.

In this circumstance, life reveals itself to us and we, as completely open beings, embrace it and understand its true value. The Reality of the moment reveals to us true life and we accept it as it comes, as something unavoidable, without reactions or psychological traumas.

Thus, we discover that, by eliminating the past as a memory, we have a completely new mind; with it we embrace only what is absolutely new, brought forth by the movement of life.

We approach pure watching in the same way. Therefore, listening and watching in this manner, we become integrated into Eternity, simultaneously with the sacrifice of the personality.

In the climate of purity, absolute Love overwhelms our whole being, offering us the most precious gift given to the man tied to this world, and that is: boundless happiness, without any cause.

A Burning Flame

What are you doing now? Where are you in the present
moment?
Are you moving? Stop, be still!
Are you preoccupied with an idea? Are you playing
its game?
Or, in utter apathy, are you absent to the present reality?
Here are a few questions we ask every day, persistently!

In order to encounter Life in its perpetual movement,
Always newness, never repeating itself,
We start from "now" – the eternal, independent,
Free from "yesterday" or "tomorrow" – a constant act
of living.

The man, free from the past, clear, lucid and watchful,
Moves the same as Life, always in the present,
Like a flame that burns ceaselessly,
Renewing itself continuously, through constant watching.

The flame which devours the old, ancient residues,
Is all-encompassing Attention; everything man
encounters
In his journey is perceived in the now.
Attention regenerates our energies, it makes us whole.

There is no other way of renewal and progress,
The moment reveals the mystery and it gives meaning
to our life!
If you are not always present, you miss your life's
purpose,
Your path is always obstructed by imaginary formulas.

When the Flame-Attention burns constantly within us,
It dissipates and disintegrates all that is ugly and
unnatural,
The erroneous baggage of the deceitful mind,
Assessing everything obsessively, according to its
own appearance.

We never stray through the thicket of life,
When the Flame is alight, the mind is completely
enlightened;
If what I say finds any echo in you,
Ask yourself these questions, so you can better
understand yourself.

If you are a whole man, in the present moment,
For only wholeness gives you the experience of essence;
You and the Sacred are "One", in perfect harmony,
This is what Life requests of you – as a source of joy!

When thought starts to fly elsewhere, you are an
                                incomplete being;
Energy is dissipated, your behavior determined by
                                old patterns,
Unable to understand that which is alive, real,
Brought forth by the flow of Life, as an integrated "Whole".

We simply watch the wandering, vagrant thought,
By exposing it, it disappears, the individual becomes
                                independent;
This meeting transforms, burns the cunning energies,
Which accompany these thoughts from ancient times.

The flame does not leave any traces, nor painful
                                impressions.
What is old and obsolete, beautiful or ugly thoughts,
They are suddenly disintegrated, without fail,
The moments succeed one another, integrated into
                                Immensity.

Through a total Attention, you persist in being a Flame,
It will light your path, it will bring eternal joy,
Even in difficult circumstances, for the clear and lucid mind
Expands into Infinity.
The whole being is inundated with Harmony and
                                Happiness!

Let us ask ourselves these questions, as often as possible:
Are we or are we not in direct contact with the Reality of
Life? Do we function as perfectly conscious beings, "now"

and "here"? Is our thinking running towards the past or projecting itself into the future?

Once we have exposed our thinking, as it wanders pointlessly on the wings of time, it obediently returns to the present, offering us moments of calm and lucidity.

The individual who is awakened to reality moves, understands and acts according to the necessities of Life on present moments, unfolding eternally. With a clear, lucid mind, he is like a Flame, burning permanently, continuously renewing itself.

All-encompassing Attention is the Flame which consumes the ancestral residues that define man as an egoistic and fearful being. Through Attention, the unity of our being is inherently accomplished and an unlimited energy suddenly becomes available to us.

Transforming action can only take place in the alive and active present, never in the future. If we are not always in the present moment, we miss Life's true meaning. The obsolete past and the imaginary future, obstructing reality through the drifting mind, will always veil the Truth.

When lucid Attention is our constant companion, we light the path of our Life and, through this light, all the residues which degrade us morally and spiritually are dissipated. It also offers us the moral capacity to not commit other errors.

Therefore, our whole work consists of watching and listening to each wandering thought, each murmur of thinking, each desire, each fear as they attract us into the thicket of time. This perfect encounter makes them disappear and, in the "psychological emptiness" ensuing spontaneously, we have a pure Consciousness integrated into Boundlessness.

In this state, we find Love without cause and boundless Happiness, which, through their nature, embellish every-

thing happening to us, good or bad, beautiful or ugly,
pleasant or unpleasant, or even extremely painful.

The Movement of Creation

Creation is movement, translated into constant newness,
Its main quality – eternal freshness;
There is no repetition and it is never immobile,
It is not the slave of time, neither limited by space.

The individual mind, no matter how cultured,
Has no access to it and cannot perceive it,
For it is always old, narrow and limited;
Everything that lives in time limits and separates.

Being connected to this mind, there is no way of
                                        understanding,
We do not know the truth about the mysterious movement.
First, our ordinary mind needs to be completely silent,
As we use it frequently, always running from one thing
                                        to another.

If we see it as it is, if we watch it wholly
With a total attention, without pursuing any ideals,
It immediately becomes calm – it becomes completely quiet;
The whole being is at peace and detached from the known.

Mind in its stillness affirms itself creatively,
It is newness each moment – man is always new and active;
It fulfills its purpose through its creative essence,
Changing meaninglessness through its transforming
power.

History tells us that in the past, through meditation,
Great sculptors or artists were seeking this state,
Able to capture something new and never seen before;
Famous works of art were created in this way.

In the same manner, inventors research for a period of time
Through their knowledge, using mind and imagination;
When they reach a dead-end – here, the mind stops,
This is the crucial moment when the new is defined.

Only newness, through newness, appears in the stillness
of the mind,
As something special, unknown before, according to its
own laws;
When thinking is passive – it is an uplifting state,
For the being, without the "self", becomes new and
creative.

Psychologically, this phenomenon demolishes the old man,
In its place, it creates a new man, in a different state
of being,
Peace and Love are intertwined in harmony,
The individual becomes more compassionate and loving.

Creation is constant movement, eternal newness and absolute freshness. It never repeats itself, it is never static and it is never caught in the trap of time and space.

The individual mind, no matter how cultured, has no access to the phenomenon of creation and cannot understand it, because the mind is always old and outdated. Each movement of this particular mind separates and limits. Thus, with such a mind, we will never, in any circumstances, be able to discover the mysteries of the movement of creation.

Therefore, this ordinary mind must be silent! But how can we make it become silent? Only in one way: when we encounter it simply and directly with the flame of Attention, without having any motives or ideals to accomplish.

If the meeting happens in the right way, the mind becomes quiet – it becomes completely silent – and in that moment our whole being is detached from the known. From then on, the vessel of consciousness, thus emptied, is able to encompass and understand the newness brought forth by the movement of life.

Therefore, a new mind, without limits and without knowledge; in its stillness, it is creative and through it, the person is always new and active. Such a mind, in a state of Pure Consciousness, creates radical changes in the structure of the ordinary man by its simple presence.

History gives us evidence that great sculptors, to accomplish their masterpieces, entered a state of meditation in order to encounter this stillness in which they captured the uniqueness of the new, something that no technique could accomplish.

The same happened in the case of great discoveries. Inventors do research for a period of time, with the help of the knowing mind as imaginative thinking, then reach a dead end where the process of thinking stops. In this crucial moment of passiveness of the mind – or psychological void – the new appears by itself, through itself, and the silent mind just reaps it and brings it to the scope of knowledge.

Often their fellow beings, even famous scholars, being limited by their own minds, do not even accept them. History proves this through countless examples. Often, inventors have been considered conmen or madmen by their contemporaries and died in poverty. Later on, after their death, others have exploited their discoveries and reaped all the benefits.

In fact, in all the subjects in this book we write about this passiveness, inviting the ordinary mind to see its powerlessness and, in humbleness, to be silent, that is to become inactive, because only in this state it becomes truly creative.

The stillness of the mind, achieved in this way, dissipates the fragmented energies of the old man, which cause and perpetuate selfishness with its many obsessive and degrading aspects.

Simultaneously, in its place, peace and Love intertwined in harmony form a different content with a different mentality, defining the intelligent man.

Let us remember, therefore, that only by detaching from the time-space structure we become complete beings, able to create in both fields: spiritual and technical.

Do Not Resist Anything!

Do not resist anything you encounter;
Thoughts, desires, emotions: just listen and watch;
They appear automatically from the baggage of our mind,
Old and countless residues, deceitful and stupid.

Everything that comes proves our true condition
As a person trapped in time, conditioned by facts,
We are ashamed of this, and we hide it under a mask,
Well adorned, trying to make it appear natural.

This camouflage is just another form, equally deceitful;
Man becomes more degraded and powerless,
The human ugliness becomes more pronounced –
Thus the world climate continues its degradation.

This is what we often encounter in the human condition,
As chained beings, misunderstanding reality;
We have inherited this, throughout time, from
                                    our ancestors
Who left behind their tumultuous thinking.

Maliciousness, cunning have been inherited from old times,
From our ancient ancestor, who became self-important
By misunderstanding and considering himself to be
                                    more special,
Different from everyone around him, as a fictitious "ego".

Today, man has become degraded, for, living externally,
He is unable to perceive his inner world.
The time is right – these times request from us
That we know the truth – how ephemeral is the "self"!

Do not resist anything! Be still, watch and listen to
All the reactions that surface and all you encounter!
No resistance to what comes in the moment,
Manifesting as inner impulses, unreal aspects.

By simply watching them, choicelessly,
They will practically disappear, through non-action,
Weakening the ego and liberating spontaneously!
The human being, Sacred in the moment, becomes
                                        completely integrated.

Can we be just mere witnesses, who watch and listen to
everything the pointless movement of the mind brings
forth, such as: thoughts, images, desires, feelings,
emotions? And, to everything that comes forth, can we
oppose no resistance, nor analyze, nor create inner
comments or assessments?

These apparitions surface automatically as reactions of
the baggage of our ancestral mind, many of them deceitful,
traumatic, hollow, without any practical value. This chaotic
and confusing flow of fantasy demonstrates who we really
are, that is, a person who lives in the dimension of time,
trapped in his memory content.

Often we are ashamed of these ghosts of the past and try
to hide them under carefully disguised masks. But the
attempt to disguise can only distort our reality even more

profoundly, for, through camouflage, the perversity of the individual accumulates within to an even greater extent and, subsequently, the general psychological climate of the whole humankind reaches even deeper aspects of degradation.

Our psychological conditioning originates from very ancient times and has reached, with the passage of time, more and more demeaning aspects.

The erroneous education we have received from the previous generation is, in fact, the synthesis of all the mistakes inherited through tradition from all our ancestors.

Both evilness, in its infinite forms, as well as cunning have been inherited from that distant ancestor who became self-important, in the sense that he deemed himself better or more special than his fellow beings, thus creating the foundation of the fictitious "ego".

Generally, nowadays people are morally more degenerated than in those times. Science, technology and culture, in their process of development, have estranged human beings even further from the reality of their inner being. More so, science and the accumulation of knowledge often degrade the person by self-admiration, vanity, pride etc.

We consider that the time of straying has reached its climax and that radical changes are needed in the psychological structure of the individual.

It is necessary that we know the truth: that this ephemeral individual is but a cartoon of a person, that the true man is immortal – divinity existent through itself – awaiting to be discovered. The divinity within us can only wait until the moment the clouds of ignorance and confusion from the surface of our consciousness are cast away and disintegrated.

This message points to what is needed to be done in order to practically accomplish this sublime endeavor. Do not resist anything! Just watch and listen to each reaction of the mind – thoughts, images, desires, fears, feelings, emotions, etc. Simply encountering them, choicelessly, leads to their spontaneous disappearance. In the emptiness thus created, the path is open; the Sacredness from the depth of our being envelops us and operates a beneficial holy transformation within ourselves.

The reality existent in each human being can only affirm itself simultaneously with the disappearance of the unreal, of the "personal self" – a fictitious and obsessive creation – holding us prisoners from times immemorial.

Eternal Youth

Eternal youth is a natural phenomenon,
It is each person's destiny – as a mature, realized
individual;
It ensues spontaneously, as an authentic experience,
An energy without support, bound by nothing.

Physically, youth depends on the number of our years,
On the body's progress towards maturity.
There are no contradictions. People consider themselves
As old as their physical age, according to their
life expectancy.

Whereas psychologically it is a different matter,
Youth is directly connected with Life's constant newness;
Life itself demands that we encounter it,
The same way She is, as absolute newness in
                                    each movement.

Without this eternal, ever-renewing youth,
We will not understand the newness of the
                                    Universal movement.
We need to have a fresh, lucid and clear mind,
Completely detached from time, from the
                                    wandering memory.

Such a state is attained naturally,
When we understand the "ego" and its powerless nature,
Unable to embrace and really comprehend
The innocence of the naked moment.

The moment makes us young, if we encounter it constantly,
Without the old "self" – based on old residues;
Youth is unrelated to time, years do not define it,
In eternal youth, everyone and everything becomes
                                    integrated.

Eternal youth is a natural phenomenon; it is the destiny of
every human being who has reached a stage of spiritual
maturity. This spiritual attainment appears spontaneously
– as a true experience – when man discovers the Reality of
his being, as immortal Divinity. In this fortunate circumstance, he has a Pure Energy and Consciousness without

dimensions or cause.

On a physical plane, youth is determined by the age of our body, by its progress towards maturity. From this point of view, there are no contradictions. People consider themselves as old as their years, according to the climate or the geographical location they live in.

On a psychological level, it is a different matter. In this circumstance, youth is closely connected to the way we integrate and welcome Life's eternal freshness.

Practically, Life itself requests us to encounter it in the same way She is – as absolute newness, with each movement. Without this Eternal Youth, we will never be able to encounter or understand the newness of the Universal movement. Only by being detached from time and space – from the wandering memory – we are able to understand that which is new and real, brought "here and now" by the constant mobility of Life.

How can we reach this eternal Youth within us? Only in one manner, that is: when we understand the "ego" and its powerless nature, unable to embrace and comprehend the purity of the present moment. When understanding occurs – as a direct experience – this fiction becomes silent, in humbleness, because it has understood its fundamental incapacity. In the "psychological void" thus created, we expand to Infinity and we acquire a new mind, perfectly functional and without limits.

Encountering the moment correctly leads us to a state of eternal Youth – without the senility based on mental accumulations. Youth is not a prisoner of time and it is not influenced by how many years old our physical body is.

In a state of complete inner freedom, on the threshold of the incoming moment – we remain untouched and just as free after the moment has passed, without recording any memory residues. We die psychologically to what has been and, simultaneously, we are reborn just as alive, fresh and always young in each second of Life in Its perpetual movement.

Mind Destroys the Body

What is the mind? What are its functions, its uses
For the individual incarnated on planet Earth?
When it is perfectly healthy – it is our guide, our compass;
Otherwise, it is harmful, destructive to the body.

We use science, technology and culture;
They are transferred from generation to generation,
                                                        by learning,
Preserved as memory, through thought and reason,
The individual can spontaneously resort to this heritage.

If we use it when necessary, in certain circumstances,
Whenever existence requests it from us,
It is truly valuable and always useful,
A reliable support and help to man.

Do we have such a free and balanced mind
Which can be silent when it is not needed anymore?
Only the wise man is a master of his mind!
Such a fortunate man functions in perfect harmony.

The others, people led by their conditioned minds,
Become mere toys, carried by the winds and whims;
The chaos present in the world is caused by this type
                                        of mind,
Through contradiction and conflicts, evilness grows.

***

When led by such a mind, what is the state of the
                                    physical body?
Without respite, it is stressed by reckless thoughts,
Negative energies frequently weaken
Its organs, senses and brain – its worldly support.

When the mind desires, hopes, pursues an achievement,
A conflict is created – between what is and the
                                    imaginary goal;
Energies confront each other, with devastating
                                    consequences,
Health deteriorates, the physical body is weakened.

Wandering pointlessly, between past and future,
Is a true disease, revealed by our inner reality;
It needs to be treated without delay
Through "Self-knowing", the only salvation.

With a lucid and all-encompassing Attention,
The mind is enlightened, disappearing instantly,
As well as its whole movement. In the "Void" that ensues,
Peace and utter silence regenerate the body.

In this favorable climate, the body starts to heal,
Health is regained, the residues are eliminated;
They have been accumulated through the poor functioning
Of the organs, stressed by the flawed limited mind.

The Realm of Happiness

What I am writing here is not a story, these are not
                                        imaginary things,
I do not repeat what I have read in a book.
In fact, I describe moments of complete happiness,
Which appear in the "psychological void" – independent
                                        from thinking.

In this "vacuum" of the mind lies the wonderful realm;
Here, the past disappears – the man – the true man,
Whole, pure and boundless, is integrated into the
                                        Universe;
They all come as a gift – by simply watching.

This direct contact with the incoming moment,
Transcends us into Infinity, without anticipating
                                        anything.
Please verify everything I say! Practice it now!
Time – as yesterday or tomorrow – does not exist.

In this direct meeting, all we need is all-encompassing
                                            Attention,
It makes us "Whole" and, as complete beings,
Without effort, struggle or mental projections,
We become one with the Absolute and with
                                            Real Happiness.

In this state, there are no problems, no conflicts,
Everything is dissipated by the Sacred Reality.
Nothing else appears in this holy Realm,
This is the purpose of our incarnation on Earth.

What I am trying to describe in this subject, as well as in all
the others, is not a product of my imagination, nor do I
repeat phenomena, stories or facts I have read in a book. I
simply describe moments of happiness, encountered directly,
from my own experience, which appear in the "psychological emptiness" or the conscious passiveness of the mind.

This wonderful realm I mention in each poem, or in its
prose version, exists in a real way and it appears naturally,
simultaneously with the unforced silence of the mind.
Here, the memorial past does not move at all, there are no
projections towards the future and, similarly, there is no
shadow of expectation.

When silence ensues, the experiencer becomes a
complete man, a perfect unity (body, mind and spirit – as
one Whole). We have a new mind, expanding into Infinity,
uniting us with the whole Universe. This summum is
attained with the help of lucid Attention, as it listens and
watches with simplicity: both the exterior world, as well as
the interior of our own being.

This direct contact occurs spontaneously, on present

moments of Life, in their eternal unfoldment. Our immediate encounter with the incoming moment transcends us into Infinity, without any anticipation or effort of will.

Everything I state here, a result of personal experience, can be accomplished by you as well. Exclude and ignore me completely, otherwise you create a theory out of my words.

In this experiment there is no time, such as yesterday or tomorrow. In this encounter, the only thing we use is an all-encompassing Attention – uniting us into a complete "Whole". From now on, as a whole being, we are one with the Absolute and we fully live the phenomenon of "Happiness", devoid of any conventionalism. Our existence in this realm, in contact with the Reality of Life, dispels any problems or conflictual states. No other problems appear, as Pure Consciousness perfectly fulfills the true meaning of our incarnation on Earth.

Melting

The Universe and I are "One",
In the "now", always.
The lived moment leaves,
The free mind is empty.

Neither past, nor future;
They cease moving arbitrarily.
The Aliveness of Life, in this moment,
Creates no reactions in me.

I see, listen and live authentically,
I become whole through Love;
In this state,
The whole being is pure.

Boundless happiness
Without images;
It is encountered in fact
In absolute silence.

Here, with the help of a few verses and in few words, I demonstrate the simplicity of the meeting with oneself, as well as the spontaneous melting into Universality. Everything happens in the span of one moment. The mind, perfectly quiet and free at the beginning of the moment, is equally silent and free when the moment ends.

Therefore, neither the past, nor the future finds any reflection in one's mind. In this circumstance, I watch, listen and live, directly, the phenomenon of Pure Presence and Pure Awareness, defined as Boundless Love.

The happiness to which every human being aspires – consciously or unconsciously – can be encountered in a real way only in the state of absolute silence. This simple, clear and all-pervading Happiness is completely devoid of any material or imaginary motivations.

Lucid Attention is the only instrument we use continuously in order to empty our mind, as well as to determine it to become silent, in humbleness.

The Fear of Aloneness

Aloneness and fear are nothing but mere words,
They are not actual phenomena, real experiences;
In fact, they exclude each other, they have no affinity,
When the state of Intelligence affirms itself.

Psychologically, being alone means freedom,
Peace, quiet, rest, as well as integrity,
Inner harmony unites us into Infinity,
Detached from space, there are no conflicts.

There are no desires, no images – all content is empty.
In such a state, the "ego" is completely silent;
We have no center and no bounds, extended into
                                        Immensity,
A timeless state, with access to the Sacredness of Life.

Fear is connected to the "self" – it never exists without it;
Everything man undertakes when he functions as "ego",
The shadow of fear pursues him constantly
And dissipates his energy through its negativity.

Therefore, fear is always connected to the finite,
                              to the limited,
Influencing the individual's thinking process;
It is always turbulent, never of any use,
Confusion, misunderstanding – its constant companions.

We ask ourselves: What do fear and aloneness have in
common?
What human weakness connects and associates them?
Can the finite and the Infinite go together?
Of course not! It is impossible! They exclude each other!

Only when the finite is silent, seeing its own
powerlessness,
Immensity appears as a natural state.
Mind has wrongly united them, intellectually,
By regarding solitude only as an idea, a concept,

And not as a Reality, transcending us into Immensity.
The "ego" is afraid of solitude, for it disintegrates it,
It is quick to fill its "void" – unwanted, unaccepted –
With any means of escape it finds available.

Therefore, when solitude affirms itself in its authenticity,
It is not something unpleasant, to be avoided or feared –
The desire to fill the "void" is the misleading factor;
The whole problem is the "ego", traumatic by nature.

When it is exposed, watched totally, as it really is,
Does it last? Does it keep moving? Attention dissolves it.
Us and the "ego" are one movement, dissipating it
spontaneously,
"Emptiness" comes on its own accord, creating a
Sacred Fulfillment.

Enveloped in Immensity, in a state of security,
Our contentment is total – there is no search, no desires;
Here all is intertwined in natural harmony,
The Sacred imposes its law, through impulses of Love.

Fear and aloneness are nothing but mere words, and not the actual phenomena or facts they are trying to express. There is no connection between these two words when the Homo sapiens functions as an intelligent being. When the mind is silent, we are outside time and we experience the state of psychological freedom.

In this circumstance, profound silence leads to the integrity of our being. The harmony of our inner being unites us with Eternity, where there are no conflicts. Similarly, in this state of "being", desires and images start to disappear and with them, the whole "ego" vanishes. There is no center of interest and no limitations. The whole being is extended into Infinity, meeting and melting with the Sacredness of Life.

On the other hand, fear is closely connected to the "self"; it affirms itself only in the presence of the ego, dissipating its energy. It follows the "self" everywhere, like a shadow, with its obvious negative effects. The individual's confusion, misunderstanding and ignorance continuously create the mournful cloth of life.

Seeing them in their reality, a question follows: What human weaknesses connect and associate fear and aloneness? Can the finite go together with the Infinite? Not at all! Because the existence of one excludes the other.

What happens when the limited, the finite becomes silent, realizing its own powerlessness? In that moment – spontaneously – Immensity appears. The mind united the two concepts at an intellectual level, for it considered aloneness only as an idea, a concept and not as a direct reality – attained through personal experience. The "ego" is constantly afraid of aloneness, because every day it disintegrates its structure.

What does this "ego" do in order to save itself? A very simple thing: it fills its aloneness with all kinds of occupations. There are various means of escape: going to the theater, to the cinema, excursions, going to stadiums, watching TV, reading books, drinking alcohol etc. Therefore, when solitude appears, it is not an unpleasant experience, something to be avoided or feared. The only problem is the "ego", misleading the ignorant.

What happens when we encounter this "ego" with a lucid Attention? Does it keep moving? Or does the flash of Attention dissipate its structure? Certainly so. The disappearance of the "ego" offers us the peace of the soul and, through it, the sacred fulfillment of our union with Divinity. From that moment on we exist as Love, Intelligence and boundless Happiness.

All Expectations are a Trap

A mental projection, pursuing a particular achievement,
A certain result, anticipated by the thinking process;
Psychologically, any expectation has its source in
                                        the "self",
Ceaselessly egocentric, in every single action.

Expectations, therefore, are a trap, they strengthen
                                        the known,
The "ego" is always present, enhancing its self-importance;
In everything it says or thinks, with each activity,
It is fed continuously; the "self" fortifies its stronghold.

When we start our journey with a purpose in mind,
We don't become free of the "ego", on the contrary,
We give it strength, amplifying it.
This is what we achieve through methods and faiths,
More and more burdened by our own powerlessness.

The climate in the world today demonstrates too well
How detrimental is effort and results achieved through
                                        thought.
The hope of being transformed has catastrophic effects,
There are pitfalls every step of the way – failure is
                                        the norm.

"Self-knowing" is a completely different path,
We start from facts, by listening and watching,
We don't have any goals – only a simple awareness
Of the Reality of Life, in perfect relaxation.

Such a simple, disinterested encounter,
Is, through itself, action and true fulfillment.
The "self" disintegrates – all traps are shattered,
Its cunning energies are gradually eliminated.

The moments encountered in this manner, persistently,
Will finally cause the great event:
The shattering of the "ego" – a state of Enlightenment;
Through it, man reaches sublime Integration.

Expectation is a mental projection, pursuing a particular result, meant to be fulfilled in a certain moment in the future. This anticipation is fueled and initiated by the structure of the "personal self", whose activity is always selfish. From the very start, expectation defines itself as a trap, enhancing the importance of the "ego".

Psychologically, every time we initiate an activity where we pursue an ideal or a goal to reach, we are merely the "ego" or "personal self" in action. Each movement will increase its dimensions, as well as its importance. This is what the ordinary man does when he resorts to methods, faiths, concepts, with a so-called spiritual goal in mind.

Spiritual becoming, as well as the faithful's hope of saving their souls as a result of effort and willpower, are and will always be true pitfalls, with deceitful, misleading effects. If we compare this activity with its results and outcome, the certainty of our statements becomes obvious and undeniable.

Can our mind produce radical transformations in itself? To this question we can answer either by looking within ourselves or by looking around us. The correct answer depends, nevertheless, on our perfect objectivity. Are we truly objective? Are we honest enough to look within and discover the masks we often resort to in order to hide our inner ugliness?

"Self-knowing" allows no compromises and no excuses. When we put it into practice, we will always start from facts – from what happens "here and now".

The simple awareness of the movement of the mind, structured in time-space, shows us clearly, accurately and without any doubts who we really are.

Such a simple and disinterested encounter is, through itself, a transformative action. The "self" dissolves, exposed by all-encompassing Attention; all the traps are shattered and the cunning energies – whose prisoners we are – will be gradually eliminated.

Our encounter with these egoic structures is realized moment to moment; we don't pursue any goal and we don't expect any results.

Such simple encounters will one day bring about the shattering of the "ego" and the fortunate individual will experience the phenomenon of Liberation or Enlightenment. A new mentality towards Life appears on its own accord, without any intervention from the knowing mind.

In the future, we will not be used by the knowing mind and its automatic reactions; instead, perfectly aware, we will use memory only to communicate and offer explanations to those who request them from us.

Practicing "Self-knowing"

In order to facilitate the correct understanding and practice of "Self-knowing", in what follows we will provide various information, ensuring the successful exploration of this whole process.

The entire experience is attained by each practitioner individually. You don't need anything or anyone else! You are endowed with all the creative will, freedom, force and strength needed for this wonderful accomplishment.

The author cannot give you any help at all. He just provides you with the information you need, as well as the description of how to put it into practice. Forget the author altogether, ignore him completely!

As you read these poems, immediately apply what they are revealing to you! Only in this way, you discover for yourselves and truly experience this reality.

Understanding appears and is revealed with perfect clarity only by detaching from everything you know – simultaneously with the disappearance of the old man, conditioned by time and space.

The recorded personal past, preserved in the memory, disappears spontaneously – Awakening happens when one becomes conscious, always new in the moment, in a perpetual now.

In order to become used to the state of Present to Present, ask yourself as often as possible: Am I or am I not awake – Here and Now – continuously in the present moment? This means of waking up – naturally followed by the Integrity of being – can be applied in every circumstance, day and night, whether you sit still or you are in movement.

Let us also mention that the cells of the body are nourished by the food we ingest and transform, through metabolism, and it is finally carried into the bloodstream; but the Life of the cells is also nourished by the energy of Thought.

This Thought can be directed, according to our desire, either to the superior state of Superconsciousness, where we live in a state of Joy, Happiness and Love; or lowered to the level of social conscience, and in this case we experience: sorrow, sadness and fear, as well as other negative effects.

By considering and practicing these suggestions, from the very beginning we will notice beneficial effects on our whole being. To name a few:

We will accept everything Life brings in our path: pleasant or unpleasant things and events, or even those deemed as disastrous.

We will not judge nor condemn anyone, no matter what they have done. We will show wise understanding towards everyone, without discrimination, for Love will lead our actions and reveal our identity as being similar to that of our fellow beings; therefore when we condemn someone, we condemn ourselves.

On the ascending journey on the Path of perfection, Thoughts become more and more subtle and will finally lead us to the phenomenon of Enlightenment. This fortunate state of being, occurring as a complete surprise, unites us with the Creative Divine – we are in It and It is within us.

All human beings are destined to reach supreme Godliness, from the very beginning of their creation. Accelerating or postponing this process depends on each entity, on what the individual thinks, affirms or puts into practice.

The fierce desire, firm determination and continuous persistence represent the foundation for this holy attainment. The means available to us, with easily noticeable beneficial and transformative effects, are: a simple State of Being, the State of Pure Consciousness, Boundless Thinking and Unconditional Love.

Each of these four states, correctly practiced and experienced moment to moment, provides the practitioner with the Integrity of being, the shattering of the "ego", the transcendence from the finite world into the Immense Eternity and the Unity with the Divine.

"Self-knowing" does not recommend nor encourages hermitism, solitude or isolation, abandoning family life or ceasing to practice a profession in society in order to earn one's living.

Such attitudes are deemed to be strictly egoic types of behavior, which flaunt the essence of morality. Living in society, the practitioner of "Self-knowing" will be a living example of high moral conduct. He will naturally influence the fellow beings in his vicinity through his honesty, uprightness and modesty.

***

From an intellectual point of view we are aware of the importance of silence; nevertheless, practicing it becomes difficult. What is the cause of this difficulty?

The "ego" is the only one to blame, for it functions as a conditioned, automatic mind. The egocentric structure perpetually feels the need to affirm itself and it does so through countless repetitions, according to its memorial images.

The mechanicalness of the mind is a disease of the human soul, overcoming our whole being with the detrimental effects mentioned earlier.

But if the mind is enveloped in the light of Attention, it stops by itself, suddenly, because at a simple glance it realizes its own deficiency. Therefore, a moment's silence offers the mind true understanding.

***

The whole secret lies in this silent watching; without any intervention from the past, it allows everything to unfold in perfect silence. Within the silent mind, a wholeness of being is realized, providing us with a huge amount of energy at our fingertips. This psychological stillness makes it possible for the practitioner to be integrated in the present and to live in a state of timelessness.

***

Each human being has the capacity to know the Absolute Truth, functioning as a Whole Man, in perfect Union with Existence; the Moment is the test which confirms whether or not we are encountering Life in Its eternal unfolding.

In this blissful communion there is no past nor future, only this moment; thus, we are connected to Life in a perfect way. This is, therefore, the Absolute Truth, encountered in the complete absence of the old man – a time-space creation, based on memory residues.

Let us come back to the significance of direct Knowing, emotional experience and surpassing the ancient, deficient condition we live in during our present state. In any situation we find ourselves, let us ask the question: Am I a Wholeness, Here and Now, present to present – body, mind and spirit?

This simple question takes us into the depth of our being and we instantly experience the simple state of Being or Pure Consciousness. Only that and nothing else! We don't anticipate anything and we have no expectations. As soon as the moment is consummated, we live the following moment in the same conditions. Therefore, Truth is experienced on successive moments, unfolding perpetually.

The simplicity of living the Truth is apparently difficult for those who are trapped in different patterns of thinking, but it is not restrictive. The experience needs persistence, toil and an extra amount of active will.

Never say: "I cannot do it!", for thus you program your own powerlessness.

Sadness

Sadness is an overwhelming state of the soul,
Also called sorrow, dejection.
It comes either as an effect to a challenge in
                                    the external world,
Or as a memory arising from our inner world.

Its apparition, its effects show us Who We Are and
                                    What We Are
In that very moment, so that we can know ourselves;
Possessed by the "ego", limited in space-time,
This state needs to be understood and dealt with.

Its causes are countless in their diversity,
They don't need to be judged or to be approached
By the very mind that created them;
This is a pointless undertaking.

In "Self-knowing" sadness disappears instantly,
When we encounter it in the moment, as it surfaces;
Attention is used to bring it into the light,
This contact dissipates it, by exposing its nature.

Sadness is not real, only a cunning hallucination,
Born out of ignorance, a spontaneous possession.
In the "Emptiness" that ensues, the sad person
Becomes a whole Divinity inside his being.

In this state, Joy inundates the depths of one's being,
                                                    effortlessly,
Peace occurs spontaneously, as a blessing
Uniting us with Life – an Eternal Creative Force.

Only in such a meeting we are united in a real way.
We discover the meaning of Life, exposing what is
                                                    unreal:
The egoic fiction, born out of straying,
A dual state of mind, based on deceit.

The Joy we encounter is with us everywhere and
                                                    all the time,
It affirms our Godliness and our creative will,
Given as legacy by the Divine, in its eternal Love,
To its Sons and Daughters, equally.

Let us acquire, through experience, the holy simple Path
And be just Sacred Presence, in eternal movement,
Such as the Divine is – an ever-changing Eternity,
We encounter the moment as new, fresh beings.

Our diligence, as well as our persistence in Being present
                                                    to present,
Immediately transports us into a State of Independence!
Thus, all methods, beliefs and systems are dissolved,
Based on patterns and fictitious conditioning.

Sadness is a state of the soul, defined by sorrow and overwhelming worry, producing negative and stressful effects both on a psychological, as well as on a physical level. It appears either as the effect of a challenge coming from the external world, or as memories arising in the interior of our being.

Such an apparition actually shows us Who We Are in that moment, so that we may recognize this state and know what we need to do about it. This particular attitude is an indication that we are possessed by the ego and that we need to understand it and solve it in the best way possible.

The factors causing this feeling are multiple and very complex – they cannot be solved at the level of our ordinary mind, because our intellectual burden is the very cause of its existence. The solution cannot be provided by the mind, for the mind cannot create a radical transformation in itself, but only superficial changes. Nevertheless, by using this modality, the sad person will eventually become even sadder.

Therefore, we need to resort to "Self-knowing", using a lucid, all-encompassing and disinterested Attention. Such a direct and immediate contact with sadness makes it disappear instantly, as it was just a momentary possession – caused by our own ignorance. As sadness disappears, the sad person collects himself in his inner being, as a United Trinity; Joy inundates his whole being. Peace and Harmony ensue as a real blessing, as he becomes One with Life on moments of existence, unfolding eternally.

Only this modality of meeting ourselves can expose and dissipate the unreal, namely the egoic fiction, as a product of our own behavioral misconception in our encounter with Life. From now on, under the influence of Joy, we affirm our Godliness and our creative force, available to us since the beginning of creation.

Therefore, let us discover, through feeling and experience, the simple State of Being, as Sacred Presence, in an eternal movement, in syntony with Life as we encounter it, with everything it brings in its flow: pleasant or unpleasant things. This is the attitude of the Divine, for it is Sacred Presence in permanent mobility!

Our ardor and persistence in being Present to Present, as a Whole Being, leads us to the State of Independence. In this way, all the different beliefs, methods, theories based on limited patterns of thinking are dissipated, unable to embrace Life in its complex unfoldment.

All the Senses are Awake

With an all-encompassing Attention, the being is present
"here and now",
All the senses are awake – Harmony is inherent;
Completely detached from all that "was", I move only
in the now,
I am "One" with Life – a potential Wholeness.

Like a burning flame, fueling itself,
I solve everything I encounter! I don't postpone it for
another time!
In such a state, there are no problems, no conflicts;
In movement, they are all resolved, if encountered
perfectly.

Intelligence and Love appear endlessly, through silence.
The Sacred within us demands it constantly
That we create a climate of peace, effortlessly,
Through this blissful encounter and perfect integration.

When the whole being is awake and completely
                                                independent,
When the limited "self" is absent, we are essential being,
"One" with the Divine – a Sacred creative force,
Help for the entire world, through our integration.

Here is another aspect of the encounter with ourselves and
I invite you to apply it straight away, in this very moment,
as you read these verses.

Using therefore an all-encompassing Attention –
without any particular goal or purpose in mind – our whole
being is present "here and now". As Attention vitalizes all
our senses – the harmony of our whole being ensues
naturally. Completely detached from the past, we move
and act only in the present, in direct contact with Life
unfolding moment to moment, as a strong, powerful
Wholeness. We are like a burning flame, fueling itself:
everything we encounter on our journey, we resolve at
once. If they are encountered correctly, neither problems
nor conflicts can continue to exist.

In the immense inner silence, Love and Intelligence
appear; they define the Real Nature of our being. The
Sacred, existent in each of us, demands that we create a
climate of peace, without making efforts through
willpower and without pursuing any goals.

The simplicity of the encounter with whatsoever the
movement of Life brings forth, leads to an integrity of

being; Divinity overwhelms us with its blessings.

When our whole being is completely awake, independent and boundless, we are creative Energy – "One" with the Great Cosmic Energy!

The chaotic world we frequently encounter on this planet will change only when each individual is transformed. And we all have the ability to allow the Perfection existent within us to perfect its holy masterpiece through us.

Fear

Our path on this Earth has ups and downs,
Sometimes the road is barricaded by all kinds of
challenges;
Sometimes, at a crossroads in our life, there are no signs.
Here comes the question, beloved travel companion:

Where to go? Which is the right direction?
We do not know! There are many hazards and the path
is dark!
We don't have intuition and courage is lacking!
But we cannot stop – Life itself rushes us!

Once, someone told us that within us is hidden
All the recorded knowing of Life on Earth;
If we knew how to access it, there would be no problems,
The wise solution would dissolve any dilemma.

Any man has access to this vast library,
For the key is within us, as well as in every human being;
There is one condition: to banish all fear,
Right now, in this moment, without delay!

Fear is an emotional state, closely connected to the "ego".
This fiction – a bizarre construction,
Fearful by nature, in all its endeavors,
Which create its structure and its frail universe.

Fear and "ego" are one – there is no duality,
Here we are, therefore, confronted with this figment
                                        of imagination;
As "ego", we are fear as well – this is our structure,
Each time we function in this state.

When either fear or the "ego" are encountered in a real
                                        way,
Without any motivations – only as a simple meeting,
It dissipates in a flash – in its place, an absolute "void"
                                        appears;
We spontaneously become immense, without beliefs or acts
                                        of will.

The inactivity of the mind – the personal mind,
Leads us to experience the Universal Mind;
Through it, the Wise man finds the path of Love,
These facts create our journey, through spontaneous action.

Only in peace, harmony, in the revelation of our being,
We will know, from experience, which is the right path.
Living on Earth – the right direction will spring from
The beauty of Love and Sacred Integrity.

Our existence on this planet has its ups and downs, successes and failures. Sometimes, because of severe hardships, the obstacles that lay on our path disorient us to such an extent that we do not know which direction to take. This confusion is caused by fear and worry, by anxiety and restlessness, by a real threatening danger or by something imaginary that might happen to us.

Here we are, therefore, completely overwhelmed by this turbulent and obsessive feeling. A natural question follows: Where should we go? Which is the right direction, delivering us from this difficulty? We do not know! There are many hazards and the path is dark! We don't have intuition and we are lacking in courage, nevertheless we cannot stop here, for Life in Its constant movement keeps taking us forward, in Its perpetual flow!

From all the literature we studied, we have learned that within us is hidden all the recorded knowing of life on Earth and that if we knew how to consult it, our problem would be instantly solved. Every human being has access to this vast library and the right key, in order to gain insight into this treasure of information, is within our abilities. There is nevertheless one condition: to banish any fear at once, now, in this moment!

Fear is an emotional state, closely connected to the "ego", whose very nature is to be fearful. Therefore, fear and the "ego" are one! There is no duality. And each time we function as "ego" – driven by a personal goal – we are fear as well. This simple discovery suddenly unites our whole being.

Thus, our real, attentive encounter with this "fear-ego", without any anticipations, makes this fiction disappear as quick as lightning. In its place, emptiness ensues – an absolute "void" – through it, we spontaneously become an immense being, without resorting to will or beliefs. We are also pure inner harmony and we live unconditional Peace absolutely.

Therefore, in the inactivity of the personal mind we find the Universal Mind, where Love and Intelligence appear and transform our human psyche. Only in the peace, harmony and serenity of the mind, through a direct experience, we will discover our true path in life, through action intertwined with Beauty, Love and Sacred Integrity.

Happiness

An intense state of contentment, a complete expansion;
Timeless being – a priceless treasure,
Accomplished by the individual through "Self-knowing",
Without making any efforts or pursuing any choices.

True happiness is without cause;
It is not based on any memorial support,
Therefore, it cannot disappear when the stimuli
                                    are missing,
Whether they are imaginary or whether they are real.

Happiness embraces everything: pain or suffering,
In Its blissful climate, all powerlessness vanishes;
It has never left us and it will always be with us,
For it is our very Nature, when we are without "ego".

Happiness appears and disappears, overshadowed by the
                                        clouds of the mind,
Just as the light of the sun is stopped in its way by the
                                        clouds in the sky.
We talk about happiness when we are, in fact, unhappy,
This is our state, as limited "egos".

We encounter it only in the present moment, in the now,
Detached from "yesterday" and "tomorrow" – as a whole
                                        and integrated man;
Thus, the mind and its causality are missing,
Intoxicated by the dimension of time, a deficient mentality.

How can we encounter happiness in a practical way?
It is impossible to find it with our mind,
On the contrary, it is an obstacle – the cause of our misery;
Therefore, the mind is the problem that needs to be solved!

With the all-encompassing Light-Attention,
We watch the mind as it unfolds in time;
Thoughts, images, desires, coming wave after wave,
Disappear in its light, for they are shadows, old habits,

Which mechanized our thinking, through repetitions,
practices,
This spontaneous flash ends all bondage.
What is left of us – a State of Pure Consciousness!
In this state – Happiness is present.

Through a "direct knowing" and "being" – as an integrated
man,
In each incoming moment, we encounter our real essence;
Our divine nature manifests itself, both as Love –
Its intrinsic quality – as well as sacred Happiness.

The Escape from the Now

Why do we reject the present, running towards yesterday
or tomorrow?
Are we aware of this escape?
The present is alive, active – absolute Reality;
All that was and will be is pure fantasy.

The escape from the present is motivated by the search
for pleasure,
In dead images of past experiences, enticing us;
Thinking – as a memory – gives them life and vitality,
But by projecting ourselves in time, they actually
exhaust us.

For the restless thought, traveling towards the past
                                        or future,
Dissipates our energy – permanently and damaging;
As incomplete beings, all we reap are sorrows
And the meaning of life passes our understanding.

Other times, the escape is materialized in actions,
We immediately try a whole range of ways to escape:
Theater, cinema, concerts, reading books, or sports,
And many others – they are mere traps we fall into.

Here, in verse, the true meaning of life is revealed,
Fulfilled only by "being", integrated in the present.
We are face to face with "what is": thought, image, desire,
It is a simple meeting – without any goal or purpose.

Nothing comes between us and what we see,
From this state, a holy action arises,
Which disintegrates all. Within us, complete silence,
When the "ego" is completely still, without merit,
                                        without guilt.

The instruments we use: watching, listening,
And a total attention, integrating us.
Through a silence without struggle, we expand into
                                        Infinity,
Here, as a new being, all conflicts are solved.

Living with the present moment we encounter Eternity
Any escape is pointless, we are united with Reality.
Life's revelations are encountered moment by moment,
This great fulfillment is intertwined with Love.

Have you ever questioned yourselves about the restlessness of your mind? Why does it desert the present and
escape, either towards a more or less distant past, or
towards the future, as a mental projection?

And one more question: Are you aware of the fact that
only the present is alive and real, in an absolute way,
whereas the past and the future are nothing else but
imaginary experiences.

We escape from the present because we do not like it,
and then resort to imaginary experiences and pleasures. In
fact, thinking, as a memory reaction, brings them to life.
And the effect can be none other than our obvious
exhaustion.

In reality, the thought that deserts the present and
travels towards yesterday or tomorrow fragments our
whole being. We are no longer an integral, complete person
and, as such, we lack the capacity to encounter the
wholeness of life.

But life, in its natural and spontaneous flow, faces us
with events whose cause we ourselves created once, in
ancient times, and now it forces us to deal with their effects.

In our current state, as incomplete beings, we can
neither understand life nor correctly encounter those
effects, as a result of our past deeds.

Other times, we escape from the now by resorting to
different temporary solutions, according to our personal
preferences. In this case, we can escape by going to the
theater, concerts, cinema, stadiums or by sitting in front of

the television screen. Others escape by reading books, developing a true passion for them. They read all kinds of books, good and bad, useful or useless. For such readers, the book is similar to a drug, filling their time, without being aware of the true purpose of life on Earth.

In this subject, the author tries to point both to the real meaning of life, as well as to what is needed in order to accomplish it. But the freedom to choose one or the other is solely yours.

In order to correctly encounter and understand life, it is necessary that we watch everything that appears on the screen of consciousness from one moment to another, such as a thought, an image, a desire, fear etc.

Nothing comes between us and what we encounter. In a practical way, we are integrated in the present, through the simplicity of the state of "being", without pursuing any purpose or ideal and without any expectations.

In this state, understanding and transformative action become one single movement, eroding the whole structure of the "ego". With the disappearance of the "ego", a beneficial peace dwells in our whole being, integrating us into Boundlessness.

Each direct meeting with the present moment transcends us into Eternity. And the joy that ensues makes any attempt to escape from the present inoperable.

We have access to the mysteries of life only in one circumstance, namely: when we function as complete beings, in perfect union with the alive and active present.

A Strange Phenomenon – The Sacred Sound

Many years ago, when the false "ego" shattered,
A sound pervaded my being, existent through itself.
Day and night, ceaselessly, it is always present,
Any external noise doesn't prevent or disturb it.

Whether I speak or I am silent, it is equally obvious,
This sound brings me, effortlessly, into the present;
The simple state of Being – a priceless Oneness,
Constantly unites me with Life in its unfoldment.

It is unlike any external sound,
Through its subtle nature – in my inner space,
It firmly imposes its holy existence,
Totally attentive, in any circumstance.

When I am not a complete man, in that present moment,
Spirit, Soul and Ego, in the eternal concrete Aliveness,
The Sacred remembrance is a great advantage,
It spontaneously leads to the wondrous Integration

Into the constant flow of Life – freshness, newness
From one moment to another – Eternal Reality.
For a long time, I considered this sound to be an ordinary
                                              phenomenon,
My hearing influenced by something inappropriate.

Finally, often being in communion with it,
I gave it its just importance and real action;
By simply listening and watching,
I was integrated in the present, in every circumstance.

When I think, speak or when I am completely silent,
The sound is united with my being, as a good friend,
Constantly reminding me of Who I really Am
On this self-created plane of illusions.

My Soul is a constant reminder, I fully live Freedom,
One with the Divine – One with Reality;
A Divine, Universal Man – Boundless Thinking,
Detached from the worldly – from Life organized
                                                                    as patterns.

Blind faiths, methods and theories, arrogant philosophies,
They are all ephemeral, transitory, disharmonic forms;
They create the mirror of Life, as they are reflected
In today's human behavior, which shows us:

That spiritually, we live in a primitive age,
The savage egocentrism is an undeniable reality.
Are we able to see all this, and what it tries to teach us?
Only by being honest with ourselves, the Sacred
                                                                    reveals all!

This phenomenon occurred more than three decades ago,
when I fully experienced the shattering of the unnatural

"ego". In that happy moment – as a complete surprise – I felt an extremely subtle sound pervading my whole being.

Since then, it has always been there, day and night, sufficient onto itself. No noise from the outside world can annihilate its presence. Whether I speak or I am silent, it is always evident. Its presence always brings me back to the present, in a simple State of Being, uniting me with the movement of Life.

This sound is unlike anything we hear in the external world. Its fineness, it subtlety creates – to put it this way – a State of hallowing Consciousness. When I function as an inner whole trinity, in the moment, this sound is a constant reminder, followed spontaneously by the fulfillment of my own Integrity.

For a period of time, I considered this sound to be an ordinary phenomenon of the auditory system, influenced by something external, such as a draft (from an open door or window).

Finally, being in constant communion with it, I became aware of its importance, by experiencing, with ease, the phenomenon of listening to or watching every reply or memory reaction. This sound is like a friend, permanently uniting my whole being, reminding me Who I Am on this self-programmed plane of illusions. With its constant reminder, I fully experience psychological Freedom, in communion with the Creative Divine, with Reality – as an Universal Man with a Boundless Mind, completely detached from everything worldly – that is, from the state of living trapped in various conventional patterns, such as faiths, methods, arrogant philosophical theories etc.

I consider all these to be fleeting, dissonant fictions – so obvious in the world we live in. They give obvious testimony of the fact that, spiritually, we still live in a savage state of primitivism and egoic behavior.

Can you see what I try to explain in these subjects, as I see it – through feeling and direct experience? Being honest with ourselves is the Right Path, opening in front of us and teaching us to look forward only, as the Sacred within us reveals.

A Cry in the Desert

With total simplicity, try to watch yourselves,
Do not resist anything you encounter.
Chase away any hopes or blind faiths to accomplish,
There are no models, ideals to be pursued.

There is no time to waste, chasing illusions,
Neither past, nor future, always be... always here.
Now is what is important – the moment is Eternity.
Show it all your respect and consideration.

Encounter directly whatever you see or hear,
Opinions and judgments are mere obstacles,
The knowledgeable person is, in reality, stupid,
He repeats dead things, which have no meaning
                                    in the now.

Look at the chaos and fear, going hand in hand,
They weave the cloth of life in this mad climate,
Your own psychological functioning creates misery,
The madness of the world has a similar pattern to that
of the individual.

The whole world is haunted by diseases and insanity,
Arrogance and pride are the fruit of stupidity;
Violence, crimes, hate and bloody wars,
Have their source in the individual and his mental
baggage.

***

This cry is heard in the world's psychic desert.
Stop the evil which threatens life itself on Earth!
You have plenty of weapons, and you are lacking in
nothing,
But you also have a powerful "ego", creating madness.

This cry-message is available to everyone.
How many of you can see its significance and urgency?
If you immediately start practicing "Self-knowing",
The whole world will change, starting from you.

The perfection of the Universe can be found
within yourself,
The only temporary obstacle is your individual mind,
Always limited, egocentric and arrogant;
Try to understand its powerless nature.

If you see it – watching totally – it disappears in a moment,
In the emptiness that ensues, there is no more movement,
Psychologically, the whole being becomes one with
Immensity;
The emptiness of the mind and the moment are gates to
Eternity.

The state of being "nothing" is an open ground for Love,
It transforms us radically, within the dimension of being.
Our present times demand this evolutionary leap,
Through radical changes in the ugly, fictitious "ego".

This subject tackles the psychological desert of the ordinary man, conditioned by time-space, whose ego-centric existence has transformed him into an unbalanced, fearful being, with a chaotic behavior.

With a lucid and all-encompassing Attention, try to watch yourself with simplicity, as often as possible, without opposing any resistance to anything you encounter. When practicing this direct experience, there are no: desires, hopes, beliefs, models to follow, goals or ideals to accomplish.

Do not waste your time chasing ghosts; these are creations of the past or the future. Persist in correctly encountering reality, offering you the benedictions of Eternity. Our whole respect must be given to the present moment.

Encounter everything you see or hear directly. In this context, it is absolutely necessary that you leave aside any opinion or prejudice, as well as your entire knowledge. The knower is and remains ignorant each time, for he repeats imaginary things, preserved in the memory – outdated in the present – which are meaningless when faced with the newness of the aliveness in its eternal movement.

Chaos, with its frequent insecurity and fear, determines our existence and the uncertain climate of our daily life, because we resort, time and again, to the memory knowledge inherited through education. The general insanity, so obvious in the world of today, is the natural effect of all individuals who approach the freshness of life in the same deficient way.

The whole world is haunted by psychological diseases; everywhere arrogance, pride and ego are prevalent – based and fueled by stupidity only. Ambition, violence, greed, hatred, crimes and wars find their support and origin only in the deceitful content of the memory.

Stop this madness with its destructive effects, threatening life itself on planet Earth! The deadly weapons expose and incite your psychological imbalance, based on the delusional and selfish "ego".

How many actually apply this message of knowing your personal mind?

Changing the world starts with ourselves, because we and the world are a "whole", and a simple transformation achieved by an element of the whole will also influence the rest.

The whole universe is within each of us and it is waiting to be discovered, but the individual, egocentric mind is a real obstacle in the way of this wonderful achievement. Therefore, when watched globally with the flame of Attention, this interfering mind disappears in a flash.

In the psychological emptiness thus created, our being expands into Infinity, integrating itself into the Great Whole. Therefore, the passiveness of the mind and the eternal moment open the gate to absolute Love which, by itself and through itself, produces radical changes in the human dimension.

Our present times request this qualitative leap on the always ascending path of moral and spiritual evolution, through a radical mutation in the structure of the ugly and hideous "ego".

Optimism and Pessimism

Optimism and pessimism – two deceitful states,
Their source is the same "ego", acting through
fragmentation;
In both circumstances, the person runs away from
what is real,
Either embellishing or smearing what is alive and present.

The optimist sees everything he encounters in
beautiful colors;
He embellishes all, what is sad becomes merry.
By thinking, he fantasizes all the time,
Turning everything into an ideal, distorting reality.

Through fictitious anticipations, he lives superficially,
Valuing his "ego", filled with empty hopes;
Continuously encouraging himself,
He cannot rest and simply observe the "self".

It is all an act, theater, with outer effects,
He lies both to himself and to the outside world;
Psychologically, morally – degradation in all
                                    circumstances,
When we distort the real, our whole life becomes an escape.

***

The pessimist is in a worse state, more degrading,
The cloth of life is in mourning.
Everything he achieves or says is filled with sadness,
What he encounters is regarded with suspicion.

From insignificant events he creates tragedies,
Amplifying and distorting them, in utter folly.
This ill-fated game sometimes ends in suicide,
The mind is unbalanced, constantly misjudging.

What fruit can be borne by a dark mind,
Always accompanied by despair?
Torment, pain and sorrow, as well as desperation;
The pessimist is defined and chained by them.

A disaster for the psyche, a shame for the human being,
A primitive, powerless soul – trapped in the "ego".
For the body: permanent stress and a premature death;
What good can such a state create?

***

Optimism and pessimism, the same deceit,
Both structures are created by a reckless mind.
Reading what I have written, what can you say about
                                                    yourself?
Do you prefer one of them, do you have any options?

You can answer this question, if you know yourself
As you really are, through a direct experience;
When encountering Life with its challenges,
The moment is the mirror of Life, leading to integration.

Only as a complete being – a harmonious Whole,
You discover Liberation, and what is needed
For this great realization – thus you find
Real Happiness through silent Love.

Both optimism as well as pessimism are deceitful states, pursued by the incomplete individual, functioning as "self", conditioned by the residues of time. In both manifestations, man distorts reality either by embellishing it or by uglifying it.

With the help of imagination, the optimist sees everything that Life brings naturally in its eternal movement in beautiful colors. Unpleasant and sad events are immediately covered by deceitful, imaginary and confusing projections. The optimist lives on the surface of his consciousness, helped by fictitious expectations, comforting him continuously with empty, hollow hopes.

In this circumstance, he continuously tries to perpetuate a vague climate of harmony, to the detriment of his own energy. It is just an act, taking place within his inner being, with effects on the external world as well. Thus, this ambitious artist both lies to himself and tries to make an impression on the outside world, in his relationships with his fellow beings. Such an approach only degrades him further; it is just an escape from the Reality of existence.

***

The pessimist is in an even worse situation, for the whole cloth of life is weaved in tears, suffering and endless sorrow. Naturally suspicious, he imagines tragedies and dramatizes completely insignificant events, exaggerating them.

Sometimes the mind, overwhelmed by stupid ideas, can lead the unfortunate pessimist to the ill-fated gesture of suicide. What kind of fruits can such a mind bear – as it is confused, ignorant and often hallucinating – except suffering, torment and despair?

There is nothing more harmful, ignorant and shameful for a human being than when, because of reckless halluci-nation, he himself creates the stressful conditions bringing his life to an untimely end! So much sorrow and venom invades your physical body, when you encounter Life with the bad habit of interpreting it through the dark vision of suspicion and uncertainty! Is this description clear enough to show you the whole stupidity of the pessimistic approach?!

***

As I had shown earlier, both optimism as well as pessimism are deceitful attitudes, degrading our whole being morally and spiritually; they also have a negative influence on the organic structure of our physical body.

When our mind is programmed by one of these options – no matter which one it is – there is only one solution, and that is: a direct Meeting with ourselves by practicing "Self-knowing". The whole being is attentive and lucid, completely open, observing the patterns of the mind directly, watching how it tries to automatically impose its pre-established attitudes in its meeting with the newness of the Aliveness in constant movement.

This correct encounter leads, inevitably, to the disappearance of the old mind and, in a state of freedom, we discover what is really useful to us. In this way we experience integrative love, uniting us with Reality and the Sublime Truth.

Being, Consciousness, Sublime

This trinity: Being, Consciousness, Sublime,
Transcends us into Infinity, we find true Life.
From this moment on, Sacredness leads our actions,
It clears our mind and makes us holy.

In any time, in any place, in complicated situations,
Everything is, at once, solved by Love,
For, in communion with Love, man is Divinity,
Kindness, Beauty and Happiness, as a Whole.

It is not an achievement – such as an ideal to fulfill
Or a goal to accomplish – in a state of duality.
Peace, complete silence is the challenge,
When the humble mind is silent, there are no expectations.

In this circumstance, we are Oneness,
We know the Eternal Reality from our own experience!
We move moment to moment – permanent newness,
We don't anticipate anything – the whole being is present.

Is it difficult? Is it easy to live present to present?
When you say "I cannot" you are the lazy "ego",
Which does not want to work, and considers comfort
And its momentary fulfillment – as true life.

Furthermore, it opposes transformation, for it dissolves
Its fragmented energies – trapped in desire and thought.
The "ego" lives through past and future, as a robotic self,
Its strength and nourishment: the constant repetition of
                                                        the old.

Wherever you are, ask yourself constantly:
Am I a Whole man, in communion with Life?
We use Attention in every circumstance,
It is a ray of Light with transformative effects.

Let us try to describe and explain the meaning of each
symbol. Being is that which is alive and in movement. We
can also call it beingness or existence, expressions used

throughout this explanation.

Being is the physical body, in deep connection with the vital or odic body; without the latter, the material body is unable to move or have a lasting existence. In the moment of death, the vital body detaches from the physical and it is dispersed into the environment. Sometimes it appears as a visible ghost, perceivable by certain sensitive persons.

Consciousness is a state of enlightenment of the mind; the moment this mind is silent, it becomes a mere mirror which, through reflection, enables us to become aware of everything around us. When we point the all-encompassing and disinterested Attention towards this mirror, it creates the state of Pure Consciousness and transcends our whole being from the finite world, uniting us with the Whole Universe.

The Sublime represents the Reality of our being, or "our divine Nature", manifested as all-encompassing Love. When we attain this supreme realization, through a direct experience, we lose our "personal self" and live in union with the Divinity.

Each time we fulfill this trinity, through actual experience, we transcend the finite dimension into Infinity and we encounter true Life. In this state we are guided by the "Divine Spark", through intuitive impulses. In any circumstance we find ourselves, even in very difficult conditions, brought about by the movement of Life, everything is solved in the happiest way possible. Being One with Divinity, we will act as kindness, beauty and Love, even in the most tragic circumstances that Life offers us. All of these happen and unfold without any intervention from our part, such as a desire, ideal, purpose, etc.

Practically, we move by connecting and disconnecting from each moment, in a permanent renewal, using virgin neuro-cerebral areas. Nothing is anticipated and we do not store any memory accumulations.

What do you say, my friend? Does this simple "being", present to present, "here and now" seem difficult?

Uttering the expression "I cannot" – belongs to the lazy "personal self", which does not like work and considers comfort as the true purpose in life. Furthermore, the "ego" opposes it, consciously or unconsciously, and often violently, because when we live in the present its fragmented energies are dispelled and dissipated. Ordinarily, these energies are continuously accumulated with the help of the robotic mind, running chaotically and pointlessly either towards the past, by feeding on dead memories – mere images in the present moment – or by projecting itself into an uncertain future, using the same pseudo-realities.

In order to facilitate the practice of "Knowing", ask yourself as often as possible: "Am I Whole, here and now, in direct contact with Life?" The frequency of this inquiry, using the Light-Attention, finally leads to the permanence of this trinity, with liberating effects. In order to enable a correct practice of this meeting with ourselves, we mention two more aspects:

The silence of the mind appears and disappears. This is its nature. We do not intervene in any way. It exposes itself effortlessly and empties its informational content and its corresponding energies. Encountering these energies with the rays of lucid Attention causes them to disperse.

The silence of being is a transformative action, realized through itself. We can also call it a state of "just being", Absolute Truth or God. In this Sublime silence or Absolute Peace, the "self" is completely missing. All attempts to describe this state make it disappear.

Therefore, the Sublime Truth, the Absolute Truth can only be encountered by experiencing It directly and

melting with It. It is indescribable and inexpressible. Any
attempt to approach it through knowledge is illusory and
it is destined to total and unavoidable failure.

How to Read and Listen to a Mirror-Poem

The title represents the subject, regarded as a whole.
You and the subject are "one" – a fulfilled unity;
The letters of the verse are mere signs, showing you
How to watch and listen to the conditioned mind.

Nothing comes between you and what you read or
                                        listen to,
Forget the author, or any kind of participation
From the thinking mind, trying to assess and reject,
Or adopt ideas from everything it encounters.

From this accumulation of knowledge, methods are
                                usually created,
Meant to be practiced, through effort and struggle;
None of these are of any use to you,
On the contrary, they are detrimental – the "self" becomes
                                even more confused.

When the mind and the heart are open, in pure innocence,
You listen or read without any purpose, yet attentively,
Without any prejudice or desire to fulfill;
Simplicity is the secret of overcoming the limited "self".

Everything the verse shows you, if it is true,
By simply listening, you become integrated;
There is nothing to be done, nothing to accomplish,
By your non-doing you have transcended into Infinity.

The merit is solely yours. The verse merely points to
How to watch in a certain manner, without any baggage.
This is what the Truth asks of you! To encounter it constantly
With a totally empty mind – independent from the past.

Each title of a mirror-poem represents a subject we try to
express in simple words, accessible to everyone. Through a
direct encounter with the title of the subject, you experience
a wholeness of being, absolutely necessary in understanding the conditioned mind.

Nothing comes between you and what you read or listen
to. Therefore, you eliminate both the author, as well as the
thinking mind who, as knowledgeable "ego", tries to assess
everything through memory reactions.

The knowledge baggage, as well as the different
methods of practice through effort and struggle, by
endlessly repeating formulas, are of no practical use to you.
These so-called values, brought back again and again into
the present moment, can only strengthen the structure of
the personal "self" and cloud the light of your own being
even further.

Therefore, the mind and the heart, as a whole being, open and in total innocence, reads or listens to the message the poem tries to convey. Both in the process of reading as well as listening, there is no purpose, such as a desire to be fulfilled.

In both cases – as the mind becomes still – if the verse is an expression of Truth, it will enter your being and integrate you into Infinity.

The merit for living these timeless moments is solely yours. Through its content, the poem did nothing but show you the way, that is – how to listen and watch without using the knowledge baggage which conditions your memory.

The absolute Truth demands that we encounter it with an innocent and humble mind, free of any previous possessions.

Only as beings who are completely free from the old past we can encounter and become one with Reality, without beginning and without end – the "Immortal Aliveness" – existent in every human being, as well as everywhere in the Sphere of Existence.

About the Author – In His Own Words

The following account is a synthesis of my life, in close connection with the initiation and in-depth study of "Self-knowing".

Until the age of 55 I never showed any inclination or felt the need to express myself in verse or prose, as it usually happens with more or less famous writers. I was just an ordinary man, conditioned by the education I received in the village where I spent my childhood. My parents, who were wealthy peasants, provided my intellectual education and offered me a good example of honesty and respect towards my fellow beings, without any discrimination.

My life, as well as theirs, was greatly influenced by the tragedy of this country and the events following the Second World War.

After a military dictatorship, somewhat justified by the interests of the unification of Romania, we were destined to suffer the most sinister tyranny that ever existed on the face of the earth, namely: the communist dictatorship.

A small minority of a few hundred communists, many of them foreign, took control of all the institutions of the state with the help of the Soviet tanks.

In my quality as a humble employee of such an institution, from very beginning I showed my hostility towards the brutal force that was taking control of the country under the direct protection of the foreign army.

Many other colleagues from my institution, as well as myself, were eventually considered to be potential enemies of the communist party. For this reason we were all declared wanted, to be imprisoned in one of the prison camps that started appearing all throughout the country.

Having been informed in time, I took refuge in the village Vartop, Dolj County, where I hid in my parents' house. Through a prophetic dream, I was warned that the secret police would be searching for me in order to arrest me. I left my hideout 2-3 minutes before the police arrived.

In those moments of maximum tension I realized, taking into account the nature of the prophetic dream, that my mysterious destiny would be also knocking on my door, as it operates according to its own laws, unknown to us human beings. The time for me to be imprisoned hadn't arrived yet. For the time being, the mystery of life in its eternal mobility and continuous freshness had something different in store for me.

From that memorable day, the 15th of August 1948, I underwent a severe self-imposed hiding regime in a kitchen attic in semi-darkness. I was 32 years old.

What could I have done in those circumstances, in a state of complete immobility?

In that extremely restricted space, forced to lie horizontally day and night, I had to start thinking about my life: everything I had or hadn't done, endless thoughts, fulfilled or unfulfilled desires, successes or failures, flimsy evaluations, vague hopes and many, many regrets. I was sick of it all!

Nevertheless, in the rare moments of total silence, something indefinite, coming from inside my being, was warning me that a change was in store, that a surprise event would happen. Still, I could not manage to understand with my mind what the hidden mystery was.

A few days after I took residence in the attic, without any warning, the unpredictable nevertheless happened.

It was a beautiful clear full moon night. Perfectly conscious and detached from my physical body, I found myself in the courtyard in front of the house, floating a few meters above the ground. I knew where my body was and I perfectly understood the circumstances surrounding the event.

At my wish, I started moving, by sliding in the air for approximately 40 meters – estimated within the physical plane. Afterwards I returned to the place where I had been initially, also by sliding, but this time moving backwards. Suddenly, an uncontrollable thought, followed by fear, ended the whole event. I felt an overwhelming euphoria, such as I had never experienced before.

This emotional state disintegrated the structure of my astral body and I returned to the attic, where my physical body was lying on the floor – as if it were dead.

I returned into my body spontaneously and naturally, without any intervention on my part. The astral form, made of small luminous dots, very similar to my physical body, took the shape of a thick chord and entered my body through the mouth, like a serpent in movement.

Simultaneously with the return of the astral matter (the astral body), my physical body came back to life. My heart was beating frantically under the impression of the surprise caused by this strange occurrence. I remembered perfectly all the events that had taken place outside the physical body, a few moments earlier.

From that moment on, my uncomfortable self-imposed prison became, without any exaggeration, a true paradise. Now I had an extraordinary occupation. By revealing this phenomenon, life had proven to me that there is no death. Armed with such certainty, I started my adventure of exploring the world after the so-called death, or the astral world, or parallel world.

I lived in this attic for over two years and six months until, eventually, I had to leave, because my parents had been chased away from the village and their house became the headquarters of local officials.

For me, this period was an opportunity of high schooling of initiation into the astral world. Dozens of experiences I had during this time revealed many mysteries that I had not known before.

Until that moment, I had never read anything about this subject. Both the phenomenon of astral journeying, as well as the discoveries I made subsequently, were real surprises to me, extraordinary facts and information.

Here are a few of these discoveries:

- When we pass into "the other world", when the final detachment from the physical body occurs, some deceased people do not even notice the effects of their so-called death. The dream is so powerful and it dominates them to such extent that, years later, they still think themselves to be in the body and on the earth. The imaginary life related to the physical plane of existence is transferred to the astral world, through the process of thinking. Sheer imagination provides a background of fictitious continuity – depending on the force of their desire and its energetic imprint.

- Thought represents the universal language in this dimension; this is how beings understand each other and communicate.

- The position in the astral world is determined by the degree of moral evolution of each individual. In my journeys, I met souls trapped for a long time in dark caves and in an unbearable climate.

- Nevertheless, I rose to the spheres of the Sublime where I listened to a divine music that has no correspondent in what we hear on the earthly plane of existence.

- During one of my countless escapes from the physical

world (described in my book "Death's Death and Liberation"), I met a group of men, women and children in the parallel world. When I saw them, a thought crossed my mind, and I asked:

"Is there anyone among you who, in their earthly existence, lived in the village Vartop?"

"Yes, there is," a man confirmed, namely himself.

"What is your name?"

"Dumitru Paun," he answered, reassuring me that he had once lived in my village.

I tried to memorize his appearance and his clothing, specific to the peasants from the end of the last century. The next day I asked my father if he knew anything regarding the existence of this man. As I was describing the astral being's clothing and appearance, my father seemed visibly moved by my account. Finally, he confessed that he knew the man I had described, adding:

"You couldn't have known him, as he died long before you were born."

This evidence was obviously meant for my father, who had probably doubted some of my previous statements.

- Also during this period of isolation, at my request, fragments of past lives were revealed to me. As far as the appearance of the astral body was concerned, I was completely different from one incarnation to another and none of them resembles my present appearance. In all my incarnations I had been a man.

- I also requested that circumstances related to the future of this existence be revealed. I traveled astrally to a very damp cell in the Secret Police Headquarters in the city of Sibiu. There, a door opened and I was introduced to a tall man. I asked him what his name was – "Faina," he answered. Another life fragment revealed in advance was related to Fagaras prison.

Within less than a year I experienced both astral predictions. Having been arrested in Brasov, I was sent to the Secret Police Headquarters in Sibiu, then to Fagaras prison. Faina was a fellow cellmate, who became a friend during my imprisonment.

- Here is another audacious experiment in the astral world, originating from the ignorance of my view at the time, as I believed everything was allowed in the world of eternal mysteries.

One day, a mischievous as well as passionate thought took over my whole being. I simply wanted to meet the All-encompassing God. With an innocent mind, detached from all worldly things, I passionately yearned for such a meeting.

Here I was, outside my physical body, being clothed in, so to speak, my astral structure. My strong desire addressed an impersonal God, asking eagerly to reveal itself to me.

A sudden vertical ascension followed, brought about by the energy of my mind. During this ascent, I performed three acts of detachment, starting with the astral body. Finally, there was nothing left of me except a luminous dot, a state of Pure Consciousness, able to see in all directions. I was part of an immense ocean of luminous dots, similar to me. Each dot was independent and had the ability to move according to his own will, just as I had the same ability. All the dots had something in common: a yellowish light. This was the end of the experiment.

The return to the body happened instantly, without any emotional outcome. I felt a state of contained joy, which was very fulfilling. In fact, this was the true state of happiness, where thoughts, desires, images etc had completely disappeared.

A few minutes later, the flawed thinking process started its pointless activity. This is what I was saying to myself, as "ego" this time: that I had seen nothing out of the ordinary, except for some luminous dots. I later realized that, apart from the physical and the odic bodies, I also left the astral, mental and spiritual bodies and reached the causal body.

Divinity was, in fact, the light that united us all within the ocean of Cosmic Energy. I will mention this Sacred Energy throughout this account, as well as in each mirror-poem, in which the real nature of our being is reflected.

I knew I would be arrested and I quickly came to terms with this idea. Both the arrest as well as the suffering that followed were written in my destiny.

In April 1951 I was arrested in my house in Brasov, then tried and condemned to 6 years of harsh imprisonment. During my imprisonment years, because of the difficult living conditions, I had few escapes in the astral world. I remember two of the most significant.

- In 1952, in Fagaras, a committee was going to separate the inmates and send them to different locations, according to the work they were meant to perform. Nobody knew where they would end up. Upon the insistence of a friend, I managed to escape into the astral and had a vision of the Saligny labor camp, at km 4. I had previously known nothing about this camp, nor about the Saligny village.

In less than 10 days we were indeed sent to this place; we labored here until the works ended in 1953.

- During this period, because of the exhausting work, I became severely anemic. I weighed only 43 kg and did not know what had become of my parents. In a perfect detachment from my physical body, I met my deceased brother and asked him to give me some news of my loved ones. This was his answer:

"Your father and mother have returned to the village and, within a week, you will receive a parcel and a letter. Do not worry, for you will be together again."

During the same week I received a parcel and a letter, confirming that my parents had returned home, as they had taken refuge in the town of Craiova. When I left prison, the second part of my brother's message also came true.

In 1956 I was released and I established my residence in Bucharest. Here, the same destiny guided me to join a spiritist circle, led by Dr. Ionel Ionescu Vladesti. He provided me with what I had wanted all along, since my first contact with the astral world: numerous books, meant to satisfy my curiosity regarding the parallel world, as well as quench my thirst for spiritual perfection. Every week I would receive such a book, which I devoured eagerly, combining reading with practice.

This circle of high spirituality was guided from the astral world by an entity who called himself Antal. He directed us in an intelligent manner, first on the mystical Christian path, through the practice of Jesus' prayer, and finally, to "Self-knowing".

At one time, this circle counted 20 people among its members. There was a great risk involved. Such spiritual interests were fiercely condemned and punished by the repression institutions of the Marxist-Leninist doctrine. But each time our astral guide gave us reassurance that nothing would happen to us, for he was protecting us. And so it was.

During this period, the number of astral escapes grew considerably. Each member of this idealist group wanted to know something about their loved ones who had gone beyond the earthly existence.

Here are a few significant aspects concerning what happens on "the other side".

- The entities dwelling on superior planes of evolution can descend to the entities dwelling below, in order to help them evolve, but the souls who are momentarily fixed on a certain plane cannot travel to higher planes.

"Here," an entity told me, "we learn as if in elementary school." The entity even had a small board; on it, he was writing instructions received from a teacher who was sitting at the desk.

- I met a woman who covered her face and body with a blanket. I asked her why she did so, and her answer was simple, "In order to sit still," and then added: "in order to gain spiritual strength."

Here, in our world, chaotic thinking runs either towards the past or towards the future, but each time it must return to the physical body. In the astral world the body is missing, causing the entity to run endlessly, exhausting one's energy to the detriment of one's own spiritual evolution.

- On another occasion, I met someone who had wanted to be incinerated after death. This man had been a doctor, an outstanding personality in the field of medicine. He was wrapped in a blanket, covering his body up to the chin. Only his head was visible. Curiosity, inspired of course by an entity from that climate, urged me to lift the blanket. I had never done such a thing before. To my surprise, the astral body, from head to toes, was completely missing.

Embarrassed by his nakedness, the poor entity was desperately shaking his head, insisting that I place the blanket back on top of him. From this encounter I learned that, through incineration, as performed in ovens with temperatures exceeding one thousand degrees, the astral body is destroyed as well. During the sudden combustion, the poor soul undergoes tremendous suffering, because the ties between the physical, etheric and astral body are still being maintained.

It is a well-known phenomenon. After death, the hair

and nails of the person keep growing, as well as other similar signs. The etheric or odic body, which animates the physical structure, still maintains its ties with it for a period of time and experiences the painful shock of incineration, transmitting it to the astral body.

After approximately two years I met him again. This time his astral body had regenerated, and it was identical to the pattern of the physical body.

- Without being asked, another inhabitant of the astral world told me: "You know, here the thieves have the keys to their own prison."

By this it is understood that those who are paying for their deeds, such as thievery, can be liberated at any time, by admitting the harm done, feeling sorry for it and deciding not to make mistakes in the future.

Generally speaking, when we pass into the other world, the Sacred within us faces us with both the wrong and the good we did during our former incarnation. And, according to what we have done, we ourselves create the corresponding environment of expiation or happiness.

Becoming aware of the harm done, followed by regret, releases us from the context of expiation. The pain of expiation is imprinted in the structure of the "personal self" and, in the next incarnation, we will err less or not at all.

The Sacred wants us to be happy. The so-called expiation is an act of love, performed with the purpose of self-perfection.

Finally, another journey into the spirit world gave me a lesson of high ethics, such as I have never encountered anywhere on our earthly plane of existence.

As I mentioned earlier, after my release from prison I studied many books on the subject of astral journeying. Among other discoveries, I learned that the sign of the cross represents a potential weapon against negative entities. I used this sign during my journeys, as priests perform it when they give a blessing.

Its effect was devastating. The sheer gesture, performed either with the right hand or the left, dispersed an entire hoard of astral entities who had surrounded me with obvious hostile intentions.

On a different occasion, I found myself in a situation where I had been immobilized by an entity, by simply raising his hand towards me. It was, in fact, an evolved soul who hadn't done me any actual harm. An inner impulse urged me to try the efficiency of the sign on this occasion as well.

In my following journeys, I used the sign of the cross many times in my always unwelcome encounters with hostile entities, which populate the astral dimensions, as well as our world. Each time I felt a somewhat feeling of satisfaction when the astral beings were dispersed.

On one occasion, surrounded by astral entities, an intuitive impulse came from within the depth of my being, urging me not to use the sign, as it was deemed an act of violence. That is, to their violence I was responding with an act of violence as well, lowering myself to their attitude.

All of a sudden, I raised my hands in a gesture of surrender and said: "My brothers, I am a human being and I have been sent into your world to meet X (and I said the name of the deceased person), please help me!

The entity in my immediate vicinity was yielding a knife above my head, ready to stab me. Suddenly he lowered his hand. After initially being aggressive, he became friendly and said to the others: "Come on, let's help him!"

They immediately took me by the hand and led me, by sliding together with the whole group, to the place where the entity I had been looking for was.

By opening my whole being to them, serenity and kindness performed a true miracle. They instantly changed their hostile attitude towards me.

This experiment had proven to me that less evolved entities – devils, as the church calls them – need our compassion, understanding and kindness and not our curses or any other acts or gestures, such as the one I was using out of ignorance.

After this wonderful lesson provided by the astral world, I realized how unsuitable, absurd and violent is the exorcism service of the Saint Basil the Great. The repeated curses uttered by priests and the energy which accompanies their words are to me something abnormal and monstrous.

I ask myself: How can the same tongue utter on the one hand blessings, and on the other hand horrifying curses?

Those so-called devils need more love and understanding from our part, because in each and every one of these less evolved fellow human beings there is the same divine spark as in the fortunate individual who has reached the spheres of the Sublime: Enlightenment.

Within each human being lies both the principle of good, as well as that of evil, manifesting itself as an egocentric and deficient "personal self". This "ego" – a fictitious structure, personal creation – is guilty of the whole human tragedy.

It brought us into our present incarnation and will continue to do so, until the day we succeed to eliminate its negative energies supporting its frail structure. In fact, this "personal ego" represents imperfection; through its chaotic straying, it overshadows the natural climate of perfection which is the reality of our being: immortal divinity, without beginning and without end.

From the very beginning, Antal, our spiritual guide,

encouraged me in my journeys into the astral world. At that moment, I had four photographs of deceased beings I had been requested to contact. Antal said to me, "Four photographs - four obligations." I promptly fulfilled these "orders", as I called them at the time. After a while, during a session, Antal asked me if I noticed any change for the better in any of the people I had given information about their departed.

"They claim to have changed," I answered.

"Leave them alone. Let them find out for themselves what they want to know!"

Under Antal's direct guidance, after trying all kinds of methods of spiritual fulfillment, I took up the practice suggested by Christian mysticism, by permanently reciting Jesus' prayer. Thus, I became a monk in the world, leading a life full of deprivations, in the hope of delivering my soul.

After two decades of fierce inner struggle, with visions of perfection, one day, completely dissatisfied with myself, I felt an inner urge to stop. It was reckoning day. My occupation as an accountant, which earned my livelihood, urged me to make an evaluation of my life. The result of this analysis was completely unsatisfactory, compared to my original aspirations.

All I had accomplished during this period were mere superficial changes, a vague cosmetic transformation that could not satisfy me. Since my first journey into the astral world, I had made a firm decision to fulfill the noble purpose of my soul and to reach that spiritual purity which I only intuited at the time.

My frail achievement, hidden under the mask of "the righteous man" – was nothing but another form of degradation – much more subtle, much more profound, but equally deceitful.

The psychological shock caused by becoming aware of

this simple and obvious fact led me to the peace of the soul and the passiveness of the mind.

When one is cornered from all sides and can't see any possibility of escape, silence comes, as well as the acceptance of one's own powerlessness. In that moment the revelation came to me. I said to myself:

"If the knowing mind, accompanied by desire, will and tension, hasn't broken the shell of my time-space conditioning – I should try to accomplish this phenomenon through the passiveness of the mind."

From that moment on I started to practice "Self-knowing" – by simply becoming aware of the reactions of the mind, with an all-encompassing Attention.

I immediately felt the effects of this practice. Simply watching the reactions of the mind dissipates its energies. I noticed that each thought, desire, image or emotion has its own energy, creating its momentum.

Within a short period of time, the constant movement of my thoughts had lost its intensity and some of my desires disappeared without leaving any trace.

These obvious undeniable effects increased my faith in this simple practice.

After a period of time, one morning as I woke up, to my amazement, I noticed that, psychologically, I was functioning completely differently than I did the night before – that is, before I went to sleep.

I was functioning as a whole – body and mind were one. The lucid and impersonal Attention gave me serenity and inner freedom, as well as energy and guidance in everything I was doing as a natural response to the present circumstances.

In conclusion, *without any conscious intervention* from my part, my mentality had radically changed.

I would like to make a parenthesis, in order to explain

how our mentality and specific way of thinking are formed, both in the case of the individual, as well as that of the collective mind.

Mentally, each individual functions as a prisoner of an educational, moral and spiritual pattern, implanted by the individual's social environment where he was born and lived his life.

Let us give a few examples: for instance, someone is born in a family of Christians; someone else is born in a family of Muslims, or Hindus or Jews; another person is born in a family where the parents have atheistic beliefs.

The family provides the young offspring with his first outlook on life. The family itself can only offer what it received through tradition from parents, grandparents and all its ancestry.

Later on comes the influence of educators, teachers, as well as that of the surrounding environment where the individual practices a professional activity, necessary in order to earn a livelihood. Simultaneously, the individual reads various books, which create continuous changes in his mentality and belief system.

All this memory baggage eventually makes up and shapes the individual's subjective approach to life.

After reading various literature, some people desert the belief system inherited from their parents and embrace another religious belief. This is just a transfer from one pattern of thinking to another, deemed superior to the previous one.

In this way, the received education transforms each individual into a genuine robot who, in his approach to life, reacts mechanically, according to his particular conditioning.

This thinking pattern, which also determines the individual's behavior, makes up the structure of the "ego" or surface consciousness; through it, he performs his relationships with his fellow beings, with nature or with the world in general.

Each human being, according to a particular education, is a prisoner and, as such, remains trapped in the shell which limits and conditions his outlook on life.

If we take a look at the various religious faiths, we can only see the way they separate fellow human beings and, furthermore, they create conflicts and enmity.

All religions and countless cults claim to possess the truth. But their own demonstration of this fact only shows how relative these beliefs are.

If any of these faiths possessed the Absolute Truth, they would not be able to function as organizations, with a hierarchic structure: at the top, the leader, who knows all the secrets and enhances his own self-importance and sense of sacredness; on the lower rungs – different levels of hierarchical importance, according to the individual's merits; at the bottom – the great crowd of believers, easily manipulated, because of their lack of understanding of the aliveness of life unfolding in the present moment.

In the historical past of life on this planet, there are plenty of examples proving the Flimsiness of different religious faiths. Killing your fellow beings just because they have a different belief than yours?! The insanity reaches infinite heights when one claims to do this in the name of God!

What kind of God urges you to hate, abuse, curse and murder human beings just like yourselves?

This cruel reality is taking place during contemporary times as well. Under our very eyes, of the so-called "civilized" man, such horrors still occur. Sometimes we ourselves take part in these conflicts, many of them fueled by spiritual leaders, who promise it will lead to the salvation of our souls.

What we state here are not mere opinions. Facts, as such, speak for themselves. They cannot be contradicted as they are clearly before our eyes, forcing us to take notice. Do not try to look away! Do not try to hide under your dark masks, used to camouflage selfish agendas, which determine your hypocritical attitude!

In the beginning of his existence, man lived in direct communion with Nature and with the totality of life in its continuous flow. Instinct guided him towards finding the things needed for survival, warning him of the perils endangering his life. This period was, of course, short-lived.

One day, a man saw a glimpse of his face mirrored on the surface of the lake. Then he looked around at his fellow beings and, to his misery, with this first self-awareness, the foundation for his "personal ego" was laid. Thus, he strayed from the guidance of Divinity, deeming himself to be "someone". With the passing of time, this "someone" started to take shape and to gain more importance. "I am more beautiful, more clever, more courageous, a better hunter and so on." The degradation became even greater with the onset of greed, the need to accumulate different physical ornaments or material goods. Adam's existence, as described in the Bible, as well as his banishment from the Garden of Eden are nothing but a symbolic account of what I outlined here.

Can you see, as well as I do, that this man, who likes to call himself "Sapiens Sapiens", has reached the peak of moral degradation during our present time, precisely because of his initial primal impulse of psychological self-importance?

Do you realize that this egoic structure is guilty of the whole tragedy characteristic of our contemporary world?

Are you aware, from your own experience (not because anyone said so), that the whole culture transmitted through tradition is deficient, because it is based on the importance of "me" and "mine"?

If you see the current evolution of things in a similar way and you are genuinely interested in the moral redemption of this chaotic world we live in, let's try together – but each for himself – discovering the Absolute Truth existent in us, as well as in each human being.

How can we set out on this inquiry? By starting from the first mistake made by that ancient ancestor I mentioned earlier.

Let's ask the first question: Are we the physical body?

No, we aren't. The physical body has a beginning, followed by a period of growth and development, then by decline, until finally, what is left of this body is a handful of earth or a few spoonfuls of ashes.

Astral journeying has proven to me, beyond any doubt, that this body is a mere cloak; as any piece of clothing, it is thrown away when it becomes old and damaged.

Are we the mind, that is, our memory baggage, which creates our psychological self-importance?

Does this mind have continuity? If it doesn't, it means that there is something else when the mind is not. Therefore, the mind does not have the characteristic of continuity. Between a thought and another, there is a pause in which the mind is completely absent.

The mind is in a state of perpetual change. What we consider valuable at one point, later we realize the same situation defines itself as meaningless, even detrimental. What we deem as truth one moment, later it becomes a lie. Both contradictory assessments belong to the mind.

In deep dreamless sleep, the mind does not exist; when we wake up again, it starts its ceaseless wandering. Above all, the mind is to blame for the whole human tragedy that can be encountered everywhere in the world.

If, during our inquiry, we eliminate the body and we eliminate this mind which, once exposed, becomes silent by itself, what do we discover?

In the peace of the soul, in the passiveness of the mind, in the psychological emptiness or stillness – who exists nevertheless? When the ordinary mind is silent, can you notice that, as silence takes over, a new mind appears, expanding into Infinity and defining itself as Pure Consciousness?

Thus we discover that we are a simple "being", "here and now", boundless – one with Infinity. In this simplicity, there are no expectations or purpose, because the "ego" has completely disappeared. This is the Absolute Truth, existent within us and everywhere around us, revealing Itself through Itself when we open its gate through a humble silence of the mind.

Such realizations, on moments of existence, operate radical transformations, eventually shattering the fortress of the "ego", whose prisoner you are as long as the mind dominates you and as long as you give it psychological importance.

When this fiction disappears, melting into the Sublime, we experience creative Intelligence, Love, Beauty and Happiness, guiding our behavior through intuitive holy impulses.

Before ending this account, I would like to mention a few details related to the phenomenon of breaking the stronghold of the "ego", marking the beginning of the psychological Liberation from the time-space dimension characteristic of the human condition.

I was 55 years old. One morning, waking up from my sleep, I noticed that, psychologically, I was functioning differently from the night before. The mind had lost its usual turmoil. In a state of serenity I had never felt before, I was functioning in perfect communion with my whole somatic structure.

My surprise was so great that it prevented me from understanding or being able to describe the mysterious phenomenon in words. I had read, of course, lots of descriptions of Enlightenment, Liberation, but there is a great difference between mere intellectual knowledge and directly experiencing the phenomenon.

Only after a couple of hours I realized what had happened to me, without pursuing this "something" as an ideal to accomplish. I was, to use a simile, in the situation of a man blind from birth, who had just gained his sight after undergoing surgery. Everything around me was as new. I had an overall perspective on things. A silent mind allows the senses to perceive things as they are.

Through silence, the mind in its totality had become an immense mirror in which the outside world was reflected. And the world I was perceiving directly through my senses revealed its own reality to me. My fellow beings, close friends or complete strangers, were being regarded indiscriminately, with a feeling of love I had never felt before.

If any reaction of the mind surfaced, it disappeared immediately in contact with the sparkle of impersonal Attention. A state of quiet and all-encompassing joy characterized me in all circumstances, whether pleasant or painful. My behavior was that of a simple witness, perfectly aware of what was happening around me, without affecting my all-encompassing state of peace.

The State of the Sublime is, of course, difficult to describe, but not impossible to experience by someone who authentically practices awareness. In order to communicate it, a simple and direct language is used, which is not filtered through reason, because the "ego", with its subjective perception, is no longer there. To put it this way: the psychological emptiness is the one who lives the present moment, expresses this encounter into words and still remains present and available to the next moment.

As a result of this direct encounter with the moment, always new and renewing itself, I felt the need, initiated and fueled by intuitive impulses, to express "Self-knowing" using verse. It was a natural thing to do. In few words I could encompass and communicate the essence of the experience.

In the first year I wrote 300 poems. Later on, their number reached 1000, of which 600 are accompanied by prose explanations, such as the ones in this book.

I would also like to describe a few effects which, as a result of becoming aware of the reactions of my own thinking process, have completely disappeared, without any other intervention from my mind.

After experiencing this phenomenon, I felt like a broken vessel, from which the following started to disappear: my interest in astral journeying, my religious beliefs, my egoism, desires, fear, envy, pride etc. My awareness remained open all the time, offering me the possibility to pass from the finite dimension into Infinity.

After encountering this extraordinary phenomenon, with the help of a global perspective I understood the whole human tragedy, caused by the misinterpretation of life in its constant mobility and newness from one moment to another.

Faced with the freshness and the aliveness of life, each individual – according to his own conditioning, as a result of wrong education – behaves completely inappropriately, because the structure of the mind cannot in any way comprehend and embrace the beauty of life. The shadow of the past is actually a memory pattern, clouding and distorting the reality of the present moment.

Life cannot be encountered and understood objectively, unless we are in a state of complete freedom and serenity of the mind. Life is newness, moment by moment, and it demands, even forces us to encounter it with a new mind, with a new brain and with new brain cells, which have not been used previously. It is a well-known fact: scientists claim that man, during the whole span of his life, uses no more than 10-15% of his brain cells and memory potential. As you can see, our psychological possibilities are almost unlimited.

After these explanations, it will be easier to understand the process of our own conditioning, as well as the phenomenon of breaking the shell of the "ego".

As I had shown previously, life demands that we encounter it directly, without any memory baggage.

How do we lose the memory baggage? It is all very simple! Here is how:

We encounter the movement of the mind with the flame of total Attention – requested by the aliveness of life in its continuous flow. Without the light and serenity provided by Attention, nothing can be understood in a real way.

In the light of Attention, any reaction of the mind (thought, image, fear, desire) – which functions chaotically, obsessively and dominates us – is instantly dissolved. In the psychological void that follows, a new mind appears, expanding into Infinity, as a state of Pure Consciousness, pure understanding as well as transformative action.

This simple state of "being" is in itself an action in which the entity who performs the action doesn't exist anymore. The old man, conditioned by his behavioral patterns, loses his authority as the chaotic, uncontrollable reactions dissolve – energies which sustain and fuel the "ego".

Only in this way, by a simple encounter with the reactions of the mind and its subsequent demise, the barrier of the "ego" is broken. Through a momentary opening, our real being is revealed, transforming and healing us.

This all-encompassing Attention, without any purpose, is the Sacred itself in action.

There is, in fact, another type of attention directed by will, which behaves subjectively by limiting itself to one object. By its very nature, this type of attention defines itself as lack of attention.

Beware, nevertheless, not to make a mere theory of this simple meeting with yourself! Simply becoming aware of "what is", of what we encounter, brought about by the flow of life, without having any purpose or expectations, places us in a state of simply "being", which transforms us by itself. That is all there is to it.

A few words about Stillness.

All that which is limited, trapped within one dimension, can be moved, according to the space available around it.

Compared to this undeniable statement, obvious to anyone, what can we affirm nevertheless about the Primordial Energy or the God present in all things – both seen or unseen, perceived or unperceivable by the human senses?

Can we affirm that God has the attribute of Stillness?

Certainly, God is Stillness, because there is no space around it to allow movement, a feature that physical objects have.

From this perspective, how else can we encounter God, other than in the peace, silence and stillness of the mind? Does this discovery help you realize the uselessness of the activity of the mind?

Happy indeed is the human being who practices the Religion of Silence – with the prayer of a humble silence of the mind!

COMING SOON

Ilie Cioara

The Wondrous Journey
Into the Depth of our Being

Published by O-Books
www.o-books.com

BOOKS

O is a symbol of the world, of oneness and unity. In different cultures it also means the "eye," symbolizing knowledge and insight. We aim to publish books that are accessible, constructive and that challenge accepted opinion, both that of academia and the "moral majority."

Our books are available in all good English language bookstores worldwide. If you don't see the book on the shelves ask the bookstore to order it for you, quoting the ISBN number and title. Alternatively you can order online (all major online retail sites carry our titles) or contact the distributor in the relevant country, listed on the copyright page.

See our website **www.o-books.net** for a full list of over 500 titles, growing by 100 a year.

And tune in to myspiritradio.com for our book review radio show, hosted by June-Elleni Laine, where you can listen to the authors discussing their books.

MySpiritRadio